To Sue

I hope .

BANK ROBBERY

BANK ROBBERY

The way we create money, and how it damages the world

Ivo Mosley

Published in this first edition in 2020 by:

Triarchy Press
Axminster, UK

www.triarchypress.net

Copyright © Ivo Mosley, 2020

A catalogue record for this book is available from the British Library.

ISBNs:
Print: 978-1-911193-64-7
ePub: 978-1-911193-65-4
pdf: 978-1-911193-66-1

Cover illustration created by Ivo Mosley from original prints by Gustav Doré.

Printed in Cornwall by TJ International Ltd.

tp

Acknowledgements

Many, many people have helped me in the making of this book, with information, advice and encouragement. They are too many to list here; but mostly, they know who they are!

Two people, however, I want to thank specifically and by name; those are my publisher, Andrew Carey, and my wife, Xanthe. They have both put in a lot of time and trouble to make this a better and more accessible book, and I thank them from the bottom of my heart. Nothing in this world is perfect, but this book has become a great deal better from their input, advice and (sometimes) insistence.

Contents

Glossary

A DRAMATIS PERSONAE OF LEGALLY SANCTIONED NON-HUMAN AGENTS AT WORK IN THE WORLD OF FINANCE.

100% Reserve. A banking system (often proposed but almost never adopted) which says that banks should not be allowed to lend more in credit than they have in reserves.

Assets. Items of property that can be fairly easily sold, if needed, to meet obligations and commitments.

Bank of Deposit. A bank that takes in money for safekeeping. Today, the term is used to refer to banks that are also *Banks of Issue*.

Bank of Issue. A bank licensed to produce notes and perhaps coins intended to circulate as money. The notes are a form of debt owed by the bank, 'payable to bearer'. Once upon a time, notes entitled a bearer to claim something valuable – usually gold or silver – but now the bearer can claim nothing except an equivalent amount in notes and/or coins.

Bank-money. Money created by banks is of a very particular type. It is legally debt owed by a bank to whoever 'owns' the money. Bank-money is created whenever a bank makes a loan: figures are simply written into a ledger. An equal amount of money disappears when the loan is repaid.

Base money. Created by governments, via their central banks or monetary authorities, it enables the whole bank-created money system to operate. Base money is the 'reserve' that banks use to pay each other and includes the cash that customers like to use in small transactions.

Bill of exchange. A written order requiring a person to pay a specific amount of money to the signatory of the bill, or to a named payee. It is a promissory note, but with a very limited circulation, so (unlike promissory notes from a commercial bank) it does not circulate as 'money'.

Blockchain. An open ledger, or accessible database, containing records of transactions in a specific currency. These transactions are therefore public knowledge. Because people are habitually secretive about what they get up to, pseudonyms are commonly used by those involved.

Bond. A form of negotiable debt, mostly issued by governments and corporations. If corporation A borrows off human B, B is given a bond – a commitment from A to pay – which B can then sell on to someone else. The corporation will then legally be in debt to the 'someone else'. A bond is a certificate of debt.

Capital. Wealth owned by a person or organisation that is not being used for day-to-day transactions or expenses and is, therefore, available for other purposes such as starting a company or investing. The word 'capital' is a source of great deception; it is supposed to originate in savings, but in fact almost all of it originates in bank loans that are created from nothing.

Capital controls. Any measure by a government, central bank, etc. to limit the flow of foreign capital into and out of the domestic economy.

Capitalism. A system where corporations and private individuals (and not the state) own a nation's assets.

Cash. Physical money held for day-to-day transactions, normally as notes and coins. In finance it is also used to refer to assets that can be converted into cash easily and immediately.

Central bank. A bank that works in close cooperation with the government, regulating the money system and providing base money (reserve) to banks of issue. It is not available for personal banking.

Charter. A document issued by a country's sovereign or legislative authority, founding or defining the rights of a city, company, university, etc.

Claim. A legal right to demand something owed by a previous agreement.

Collateral. A valuable asset held as security for a debt; a debtor who is unable to pay surrenders the collateral.

Collateralised debt obligation (CDO). A way of deceptively creating value, and of exchanging debt for cash. Large amounts of debt are gathered together, some dubious some not, and claims to the total are sold for money. CDOs were widely blamed for the 2008 crash.

Commercial bank. A bank (unlike a *merchant bank*) where most people do their banking. Their main function in the economy is to create the money supply (as debt owed by themselves) under the auspices of the government. Often used interchangeably with *Bank of Deposit*.

Commodity. A raw material or agricultural product, especially in the form in which it can be bought, sold or traded.

Community currency. A type of *Complementary currency* used by groups with a common bond, like members of a locality. Its main contribution is to encourage spending at local businesses, so money remains circulating in the community rather than being siphoned off to remote owners.

Complementary currency (CC). Exists alongside a national currency and is usually set up for an ideological or practical purpose. The great variety of these purposes is reflected in the great variety of CCs. The dominance of debt-based currencies means that CCs are somewhat tenuous – unless they benefit some powerful organised entity which can protect them.

Compound interest. When unpaid interest is added to a debt, the debt grows and the interest demands grow too. Both will grow exponentially.

Corporation. A working group given (by law) most of the rights of a human being and devoted to maximising profits for its owners.

Cosmopolitical. An ideology that sees all human beings as belonging to a single community, based on a shared morality.

Credit. Debt lent at interest that circulates as money.

Credit-clearing. *Bank-money* represents debt owed by a bank to an individual. Banks do not pay out on these debts to individuals, but when a payment is made to a customer at a different bank, the first bank will owe the second bank 'reserve'. Banks owe each other large amounts of money. These debts can mostly be set off against each other and this process of setting-off is called credit-clearing.

Credit default swap (CDS). In return for regular payments from a creditor, a third party takes responsibility for paying a debt if the debtor fails to pay.

Credit rating. Global debts are worth more than three times global production, making debt the principal item of value in the world today. Some debts are worthless as the debtor hasn't enough assets to pay; others are solid. A huge business sector rates 'credit-worthiness' in individuals and organisations, so the re-sale value of what they owe may be assessed.

Debt jubilee. The idea of occasionally cancelling all debts originated in ancient Mesopotamia. Rulers needed popularity; they needed free and independent citizens to act as soldiers; and they needed restraints on professional lenders becoming too powerful.

Debt slavery. The ultimate way of repaying a debt. If a debt was unpaid, the creditor could claim the person and family of the debtor to sell as slaves, or to profit from their labour, to get his money back.

Deposits. Deposits can be created by a genuine deposit of already existing money; or they can be created when a loan is made: the bank merely writes numbers into an account and loans out those valuable numbers – which become money because the law says they can be money.

Deregulation. Regulations were introduced into the *bank-money* system when it became clear that systemically-created dangers (like inflation and cycles of boom-and-bust) needed to be guarded against. 'Deregulation' means the removal of many of these restraints, since when debt-creation has grown into an industry larger than all other industries put together.

Derivative. A form of created debt consisting of claims on assets or groups of assets. The claims may be greater in volume and value than the assets supposed to support them; in this way they are a creation of value, similar to *bank-money*.

Digital currency. A specific type of created currency (the term is often used interchangeably with 'cryptocurrency' and 'virtual currency'). Since experts disagree on definitions, it seems best to avoid the term and be more specific.

Distributed (or open) ledger. A database shared and synchronised across multiple sites or institutions, which allows transactions to have public 'witnesses' and makes cyberattacks more difficult. The participant at each node of the network can access the recordings shared across that network and own identical copies. At present, such ledgers are used mostly for virtual currencies such as *blockchain*.

Equity. In financial usage, the legally-recognised ownership of some proportion of a business or other property.

Exchange. Today, a marketplace where securities, *commodities, derivatives*, etc. are traded. In the past, a place where currencies could be exchanged for each other and for gold and silver. According to banking historians, modern banking originated in exchanges (not money-lending).

Federal Bank. In most countries, the federal bank is a bank owned by the central or federal government. Usually it acts as a *central bank*.

Feudalism. A system in which those who worked on the land were bound to do military service for those who owned the land, to pay them rent with a certain proportion of their produce, and to do specified work for them.

Financial services. People and organisations who work to increase the assets of others. Much of this is done by trading in the various forms of debt that now dominate the world marketplace.

Fiscal. Relating to government finance: taxation, income and public spending.

Fractional reserve banking. When banks create a great deal more in credit than they have in cash and *reserve*. The system supports today's capitalism. It is why banks go bust if everyone turns up at once to claim the cash owed to them – unless, of course, the government immediately supplies banks with more 'reserve'. This is easy to do, now that 'reserve' is not gold but mere numbers.

High-powered money. Another term for *base money* or *reserve*. Ten times, twenty times or even more *bank-money* may be created on the back of a single quantity of government-created high-powered money.

Humanism. A belief that humanity can progress in justice, mutual respect and freedom without the need for a belief in God.

In-bank payment or **intra-bank payment**. A transfer of money between two accounts at the same bank. It is the very essence of debt becoming a form of money: the bank owes first one person, then another after the payment is made. Debt is transferred.

Inflation. When a given amount of money is able to buy less and less. It happens when new money is created in large amounts, unrelated to growth (or shrinkage) in the size of the economy. Inflation devalues genuine savings.

Interest. Money paid regularly in return for the use of money lent, or for delaying the repayment of a debt. Interest rates must be kept low when the world is awash with debt, or many people would go bankrupt.

IOU. Abbreviated from the phrase 'I owe you' and signifying a debt agreement between two persons, formal or informal.

Joint stock company. A company whose shares can be bought and sold.

Legal tender. Money recognised by a country's legal system as valid for meeting a financial obligation. Effectively: if you've paid for something in legal tender, you can't be sued for failing to pay. What is recognised as legal tender varies greatly from one legal jurisdiction to another.

Leverage. When an asset is used as collateral to borrow a much larger sum to finance or expand operations. So called because it is like using a lever to shift a large object. When debt is made negotiable, it becomes much easier for a company to borrow and grow larger; therefore, *negotiable debt* laws favour large concentrations of power, monopolies, etc.

Licence. Usually, a business may not use words like 'bank', 'insurance' or 'national' in its name, unless it holds a corresponding licence.

Merchant bank. Unlike *commercial banks*, a merchant bank does not create money. It offers underwriting, loan, financial advising and fundraising services for large corporations and high net worth individuals. It does not provide regular banking services to the public.

Money-creation. Money can be created in many ways. The main method today is for a bank to write new numbers into a ledger and to lend out these numbers. The numbers represent what the bank owes, first to the borrower and then to subsequent payees. This is why most money is today, in reality, debt from banks.

Money-market funds: pools of money collected from many investors and then invested (by fund-managers) in assets that are stable and can be easily sold. Such investments are as safe as deposit accounts in banks, but they yield more income.

Money-power. A term used during the (historical) transition away from feudal-based power, to denote the power and influence of a new class centred on enterprise, trade, finance and capital.

National bank of credit. A state-owned bank operating alongside (and in the same manner as) commercial banks. Instead of lending purely for profit, it lends to projects with a social benefit. Banking profits go to governments, thereby reducing taxation.

National Debt (aka public debt). Governments borrow in the name of their citizens, who are obliged to supply interest payments – usually via taxation. Because debt is negotiable, the lender receives a bond in exchange which is (initially) as valuable as the money lent; so the lender is no worse off after lending.

Near-money. Assets that can quickly and easily be converted into cash or *bank-money*, e.g. government debt (*bonds*) and *money-market funds*.

Negotiable debt. Debt that can be bought and sold. Also called tradeable, transferable, commodified or assignable debt, or circulating credit.

Non-bank Payment Service Provider. PSPs have grown in number and importance in international payments. They introduce a worry: when money is mostly numbers in ledgers, opportunities for fraud are great. This is especially true when money-numbers are created by private institutions and when regulatory bodies differ greatly between legal jurisdictions.

Plutocracy. A nation or society in which rich people hold the most meaningful and pervasive forms of power.

Price and wage controls. When a country is experiencing out-of-control inflation, it may put a ceiling on wages and prices to curb the inflation.

Projector. A term mostly used in the early 18th century, meaning an inventor and/or promoter of dubious schemes, supposedly to benefit humanity (but actually more often to benefit themselves).

Promissory Note. A written note promising to pay a stated sum to a specified person at a specified date, or on demand. Bank-notes are promissory notes. The key moment in the global development of banking was when banks' promissory notes were made legally transferable from one person to another (see below).

Promissory Notes Act 1704. Until this Act was passed, no one could be sure whether the law would enforce payment of a debt to someone who had not actually lent the money. So promissory notes could not securely be used as money, still valid after changing hands. The Act provided the legal prerequisites for promissory notes – and debt generally – to become valuable commodities. It was subsequently copied throughout the world.

Pure money. Pure money is not created as debt, nor is it created by being lent out at interest; it exists as property pure and simple. Pure money is more permanent than debt-based money, which is continually being 'retired' and re-created. Pure money can take any form that is secure and protected in law. For many centuries, gold circulated as pure money.

Reciprocal debt. Created when two parties agree to owe each other an identical amount: the two debts can be created from nothing. If debt is legally negotiable at the time, and the two parties are both wealthy, then both debts will be valuable commodities.

Repo. A repurchase agreement whereby A sells something to B and at the same time agrees to buy it back later at a higher price. Both parties are expecting to profit; A from using the money, B from the price difference.

Reserve. Digits supplied by governments to banks. When customers make payments between different banks, the banks settle their debts to each other in 'reserve' digits. Reserve digits are also the basis of cash. Reserve is also called 'high powered money', 'base money' and 'central bank money'.

Revolving door. The movement of people between jobs as legislators or regulators, and jobs in the industries affected by the legislation and regulation. The phrase implies a conflict of interest.

Shadow banking. Lending and other financial activities carried out by unregulated institutions or under unregulated conditions. It enables *money-creation* to flourish outside the regulatory system, and ratios of credit to assets to balloon, increasing both inequality and risk.

Sovereign money. A term used by those interested in monetary reform to refer to money issued by the state. It usually implies that such money is not issued as a form of debt but is intended for permanent circulation, and so is a form of *pure money*.

Special drawing rights (SDRs). A form of international money designed by the IMF as an intermediate currency but made insignificant by the continuing dominance of the US dollar.

Specie. The old name for gold, silver and other precious metals when used as raw material for coinage. Today, it can also mean money in coin form.

Speculator. One who buys an asset hoping to profit from a rise in its price.

Surplus value. When workers produce more than is necessary for their survival, the extra is referred to as surplus value. This extra tends to be seized by others who have the legal means or the power to do so.

Tax-farming. A system where governments give private individuals or corporations the power to collect taxes and allow the use of force and violence to collect them. The apparatus of state violence may be allocated to assist collection.

Unbacked. In the context of this book, a claim or debt which a debtor does not have the means to pay off fully.

Unit of Account. A measure used to compare the values of different items, often described as one of the primary functions of money.

Usury. Originally the lending of money at interest, which religions tended to disapprove of. Once the *money-power* became dominant, its meaning shifted towards 'lending money at excessive rates of interest'.

Zero-sum game. A process where when someone gains, someone else must lose an equal amount. In a zero-sum game, value is not created, so nothing is taken from (or given to) the population at large.

Introduction

Like a lot of people, I woke up a decade or so ago and noticed that many things in this world were getting worse rather than better, with serious implications for all our futures. Looking for explanations, it seemed that a lot of these things relate to how power is concentrated in large organisations which don't necessarily have our best interests at heart.

Looking further, I saw these powers getting their strength and lack of accountability from a single source: from the way money is created, rented out, cancelled and re-created for those who already have money and power. This system feeds war, climate change, inequality, the degradation of our planet, and many other evils that contaminate our present and threaten our future (see Chapter Seven). It seemed to be the most important single element in the ongoing destruction of our world, but also the least talked about and the least widely known about.

I wanted to read a simply-written book that would tell the story of how money-creation works and how it came to be. I couldn't find one, so I investigated further and decided I'd try to write it myself. Many years later, here it is. It is not an attack on individuals or a rant against bankers. It is an examination of a system that supports unaccountable and destructive power, and it is also a pointer to simple reforms that are necessary if we wish to create a more just and equitable world.

Because the story of how money is created, destroyed and re-created today is unfamiliar to most people, there will be a certain amount of repetition in the book. It also seems a good idea to give a summary of the basics here. (This account is no invention; the essential details can be checked by reading *Quarterly Bulletin 2014 Q1* on the Bank of England website.)

Money today is mostly (consistently over 90%) numbers in bank accounts. Banks create this money when they loan it.[1] They create it by simply writing a number into a customer's account, and this number becomes money. The money is a loan to the customer; it is rented out at

---

[1] "Most money in the modern economy is in the form of bank deposits, which are created by commercial banks themselves." (Bank of England, 2014)

interest. As the customer makes payments to other people, so the sum divides into smaller amounts and circulates as money.

When a loan is made, both parties – bank and borrower – expect to make a profit and have calculated they will get one. The bank expects interest on the loan: the borrower's profits must be extracted elsewhere and more than cover interest payments.

When the loan is repaid, the numbers are cancelled out and an identical amount of money simply ceases to exist. New money is soon created to replace it, however, because that is how banks make *their* income.

This method of creating and managing the money supply advantages those who use it: corporations, governments and individuals chasing money and power. It is no exaggeration to say that the unaccountable powers created by this system underpin the multiple forms of crisis that the world is facing today.

Take inequality, for instance. Our method of creating money contributes to the exploitation of productive workers in a very simple way. With new borrowed money, 'capitalists' buy up assets – property, businesses, land, etc. – and make things 'more efficient', which in practice means increasing profits by reducing costs. This is done in a number of ways: 'unnecessary' workers are shed, the workload for others increases. Downward pressure is exerted on wages and on prices for supply. Lawmakers are influenced to pass favourable legislation. Taxes are avoided. Legal loopholes are exploited. Markets are monopolised. Where advantage can be bought, corrupt payments are made. These are just a few examples of how profits are increased in the name of 'efficiency'. The costs of these profits fall on others: workers, taxpayers, society at large.

When the work of 'streamlining' is done and profits are taken, the initial borrowing is paid back to the bank. The money repaid no longer exists, but as I mentioned earlier more will soon be re-created for another profit-taking venture. The system enables huge amounts of money to be created, destroyed, and re-created, always for the profit of banks, 'capitalists' and governments. The profits go into huge accumulations that lie in wait for other profitable opportunities. The process helps to create the vast gulfs of inequality which influence daily living in our world.

Money does not have to be created, rented out and destroyed in this way. Money can be – and historically often has been – something that just circulates and is permanent: in other words, it can be like most of us imagine it is. Only when financial and political players become fully intertwined are laws passed to make our present method of creating money possible. The laws that enable it are very specific (see Chapter Two) and always the results have been disastrous (see Chapter Eight).

It's time to change things now if we want humanity to flourish much longer on this earth. Already, powerful individuals are designing rockets to take them to other planets when they're done with this one. These other human-friendly planets are, of course, fantasies; they don't exist. And even if you fancy a trip to nowhere, there won't be many places on board!

Common Illusions about Banks and Bankers

Two common illusions about banks and finance need addressing at once.

The first is that, behind the scenes, bankers pull the strings and 'run the show'. This is wrong. The system gives power to individuals, corporations and political powers, and *they* run the show – because we have become dependent upon them for our daily bread.

States, and their legislatures, give banks the power to create money by passing laws. They pass these laws because the way banks create money increases power for the state as well as for other powerful entities such as corporations. These laws are simple: they allow debt to be bought and sold as a commodity (see Chapter Two). The same laws that allow banks to create money also make it easy for states to borrow by creating their own brand of negotiable debt – bonds – which can be freely bought and sold.

When debt can be bought and sold, it is called 'negotiable'. Negotiable debt cements the alliance between wealth and power. I include here a paragraph written by the economist Luciano Pezzolo explaining the attractions of negotiable debt for those who seek power. I have taken the liberty of translating it from 'economese' into simple, ordinary English.

> Negotiable debt is not just a way of oppressing the lower classes. It has other functions too. Firstly, by creating large concentrations of capital, it allows governments to create military power and to exercise control over wide areas. Secondly, it involves wealthy people in government where they all profit together. Third, it creates a system of dependence, poor on rich, that ensures social stability. Fourth, when debt itself becomes money, a huge variety of speculative techniques is opened for the wealthy to increase their wealth. Lastly, negotiable debt enables governments to reward their supporters with stable and long-lasting incomes. (Goetzmann, 2004: 163)

In these ways, negotiable debt increases a nation's economic capacity for war-making and the ruling class's ability to profit from workers. Today, war, robbery and exploitation are (in theory) looked on askance; in fact, they carry on, administered by a system which is protected by the fact that few people understand it.

The money system favours large concentrations of power, taking surplus value out of local communities – in the form of money – off to remote ownership. This money is then put to work to extract more. Thus the system takes wealth from local communities and makes them more dependent on remote powers (see Chapter Seven).

Not only that; the activities of the powerful are putting our whole world in jeopardy. It is surely time for 'the people' – ordinary citizens – to have a greater say in the management of world affairs. For this to happen, the main instrument of oppression and exploitation – negotiable debt – should be dispensed with.

A second illusion about finance, which infects extreme left and extreme right on the political spectrum, is that 'the Jews' are somehow responsible for banking and capitalism. This fantasy, which in hard times is subtly encouraged by politicians on both 'left' and 'right', conveniently distracts blame from the true architects of the system, which are the powers of state, law, and individuals with insatiable appetites for wealth and power. As the situation today worsens, it seems important to address this delusion. All serious historians of banking have felt obliged to address it.[2]

The tradition of 'deposit' banking goes back to Ancient Mesopotamia and has come to its dominance in the world today via ancient Greece and Rome, medieval Italy and the Lombards, the Dutch, the English, the Germans and the Americans. In all these civilisations, Jews were historically marginalised and excluded from 'deposit' banking, the kind of banking which creates money as credit. In modern history, this exclusion was reinforced by a requirement to take Christian oaths.

'Merchant' banking, which was traditionally allowed to Jews, does not create money. It is a form of money-lending; the money has to exist before it is lent. The system that dominates and exploits our world today is not

---

[2] For instance, Raymond de Roover (1963): "[Jews] confined their activities to money-lending on a small scale and the leading international bankers, such as the Medici or the Fuggers, were all Christians. There is, therefore, nothing to support Sombart's thesis according to which the Jews were the originators of international finance and the founders of modern capitalism."

money-lending but 'deposit' banking – a continuous cycle of creating, renting out, destroying and re-creating money for power and profit.

Conspiracy theories blaming abuses of power on individuals are mostly wide of the mark. In reality, ruling classes make laws that advantage themselves. These laws create systems, which become the familiar backdrop to everyday life. They survive unquestioned by most people (who have to get on with living) and are exploited by those they favour. This is the case with bank-money today.

Reform

When the money story comes together, it points to a simple way of reforming things *on paper*. Reform will be hard, however, to achieve in practice because powerful people will not want to give up the source of their power. Our money system was established by passing some simple laws (see Chapter Two). The simple approach to reform is to rescind them (see Chapter Nine). Some will object that a reformed money system will prevent governments undertaking important infrastructure projects such as roads, hospitals, modernisation. This is not true: governments could still tax, borrow and create money within limits. More importantly, society itself would be more affluent and less corrupted by criminality and greed: wealthy people would pay their taxes! Almost everyone would be better off; life would be more comfortable and less lived-on-the-edge; government expenditure would be more open and accountable.

The money system was designed for theft on a grand scale. It originated at a time when theft on a grand scale – war and empire-building – was thought glorious. Theft on a small scale, of course, was punishable by death! Our money system is a toxic left-over from that time.

Today, we are trying to move on from theft as a way of life, but the way money is created makes it hard for us to change our behaviour. Opportunities and temptations built into the system encourage the worst in us (and the worst among us) to prosper.

The book finishes with a simple suggestion for reform. In a sentence, what we to end negotiable debt: to end laws that enable money and other valuable debt to be created out of nothing. In ordinary language, this means returning to a time when debt could not be bought and sold as if it was a commodity like burgers or beans (see Chapter Nine).

Only then can we begin to move on towards a more civilised future.

CHAPTER ONE

The Money Supply: How it Came to be Created by Banks

A Few Words about Money

Money is our name for whatever circulates as a way of paying for things. Money can take many forms: among these forms today are coins, notes and numbers in bank accounts. In other societies, money has been shells, tobacco, carved stones, salt and many different things.

From the point of view of human happiness and justice, the physical form that money takes is not its most important feature. Its most important feature is whether it circulates without interference and manipulation, doing only its work of facilitating buying and selling; or whether it is created and rented out by political and financial powers for their own benefit and gain. In other words: are our transactions made on a just and level playing field, or is the money supply structured to favour those who chase power?

The words 'I promise to pay' on many banknotes are an indication of how money has become an item to be created and rented out. A 'promise to pay' is a debt; the banknote represents a debt. Today, all money is issued as debt owed by a bank, central or commercial, and at the same time a corresponding debt is created for the party to whom it is issued. This complex-seeming arrangement will become clearer as the chapter progresses.

Money and Power

Because money can buy almost anything, control of the money supply is an obvious goal for anyone who wants to become massively wealthy and/or powerful. But getting control is only a beginning. How to use the money supply to make money for oneself is the real challenge.

Very early on in history, a simple way of doing this emerged. When money was gold and silver, palaces and temples in ancient Mesopotamia hoarded the gold and silver. These institutions wrote out promises-to-pay (equivalent to today's bank notes) on clay tablets. Some of these clay tablets were given out in exchange for deposits of gold and silver, while others (it seems) were rented out at interest. They might circulate, making payments, and be eventually repaid without any gold or silver leaving the temples or palaces. In other words, the tablets themselves became money. This is the essence of modern banking – invented five thousand or more years ago![3]

These clay tablets, promising to pay a certain amount of money, were in legal terms a form of debt, signifying that the temple or palace bank owed the owner of the tablet some gold or silver.

This innovation meant there were two kinds of money in circulation. There was money consisting of gold and silver – in today's terminology, 'cash' *(see glossary)* and there were clay tablets promising to pay out 'cash' – in today's terminology, these were notes of 'credit'. Credit is debt owed by a bank and lent at interest. The bank, of course, gets the interest.

Debt lent at interest! This idea still seems strange and unfamiliar – even though it has dominated the world of wealth and power on and off for thousands of years. There will be more on how the system works today in Chapter Three.

~ ~

---

[3] "After this principle was once discovered, its advantages and benefits were found to be so manifold that nothing could stay its victorious advance." (Pruessner, 1928)

Our two-tier system of cash and credit is thus very ancient. It has emerged again and again in history, always helping to integrate political power and wealth. It also held some advantages: large payments could be made by transferring credit, much safer and easier than transporting heavy metal. This advantage is now no longer relevant: with new technology, payments can be made efficiently and easily within digital payment systems.

Eventually, two-tier banking systems have always led to breakdown in civilisation, as inequalities of power and wealth become intolerable and destructive. After that, the two-tier system disappears along with the civilisation it has corrupted – until it re-emerges, when a government once again passes laws enabling credit to circulate as money (see Chapter Eight).

For a very long time, 'cash' in these two-tier systems was something valuable in itself – usually gold or silver. Then, under stress of war, governments began substituting their own promises-to-pay – their own 'credit' – for gold or silver when it was in short supply. (In Britain, this first happened in the late 18th century: 1797, to be exact).

Eventually, in the 20th century, gold and silver were dispensed with entirely and replaced with credit supplied by the government. As a result, our two-tier system is now made up of two different kinds of credit. Firstly, what we call 'cash' is in fact credit created by the government or central bank – 'promises-to-pay' in the form of notes and coins. Secondly, 'money in the bank' is in fact credit created by commercial banks.

Notes and coins – today's 'cash' – are supplied on demand by banks to customers in exchange for numbers in their bank accounts. The bank rents these notes and coins from the central bank along with 'reserve' – this arrangement will be explained in Chapter Two. The two-tier system is a collaborative venture between government and private finance, taking profit from productive/contributive citizens.

So, today's entire money supply is created as debt. The debt is somewhat theoretical: since the debt is itself money, it need pay out nothing but itself. Customers do not feel cheated, because money is after all what they want.

The magic trick of bank-money-creation occurs when a bank lends. Two debts are created simultaneously, merely by writing numbers into an account. One debt is from the borrower to the bank, the other is from the bank to the borrower. They are reciprocal debts: they add up to nothing, they come from nothing, and they will return to nothing when the customer's debt is repaid. There is nothing 'theoretical' about this second debt, however: it must be repaid, with interest, back to the bank.

The debt from the bank, however, is probably best called 'fake debt' for two reasons: because interest goes to the debtor (the bank), and because the debtor need never pay out anything valuable to the other party, other than the debt itself.[4]

Commercial bank-credit means that as payments are made in the outside world, in fake debt, the bank (theoretically) owes money first to one person and then to another. In the words of an economist, "a bank is in the delightful position of living on the interest of what it owes" (Graham, 1936). The debt owed by the customer, on the other hand, is ordinary debt and must be repaid along with interest.

Because the debt from the bank is money, and money is valuable, it seems quite fair that we pay to borrow it. This hides the real injustice in the system, which is not the payment of interest. The real injustice spreads far and wide but begins with two simple facts: money is created out of nothing for profiteers, and the entire money system is rented out at interest.

After new money is created, and until it is cancelled, it behaves as we expect it to, passing from person to person in payment for things. This diverts the public from noticing how the money system contributes (as already mentioned) to so many bad things: huge inequality, proliferation of weapons, ecological destruction, and the powers of vast, badly-behaved corporations. These subjects are explored in Chapter Seven.

A practical narrative illustrates how the system emerged and evolved quite easily and naturally from the simple practice of bankers storing money for clients – a practice innocent enough in itself, but almost inviting corruption. Breaking the process down into stages makes it easy to understand how banks came, with the help of governments and central banks, to create almost all – over 90% - of the world's money supply.

~ ~

Some of the earliest forms of writing that survive today are not literature or law or religious stories, but records on clay tablets of how much is owed by someone to someone else. This, for instance, was written on a tablet in Mesopotamia several thousand years ago:

---

[4] A bank will, however, have to make payments of 'reserve' to other banks when its debt passes into general circulation: this point is covered in Chapter Three.

> Mannu-ki-Ahi and Babu-Asherad acknowledge they have 10 minas of silver belonging to Remanni-Adad, chariot-driver, at their disposal. (Van de Mieroop, 1999: 19)

This is banking in its simplest and most innocent form. A person (in this case, the chariot-driver Remanni-Adad) leaves money with two bankers for safekeeping and gets a credit note (in this case, a clay tablet) in return. Temples in ancient Sumer, Babylon, Egypt, Greece and Rome stored money for people: they were religious institutions doubling up as banks – or was it the other way around?

There is obviously a big difference between bankers storing money and bankers *creating* money. So, how did banking evolve from simply storing money to creating it? Staying with Remanni-Adad and his bankers for a moment, we can see the simple stages in this evolution, and eventually how 'money' became ' debt owed by a bank'.

The first stage is to imagine you are a temple banker. With all that cash sitting around, and people happy to leave it there, you think 'Why not put some of it to use?' – by lending, investing, or simply spending it. Every so often someone will ask for 'their' cash, so you mustn't lend or spend *all* of it. Part of a banker's skill is to judge how much they should keep handy and how much they can get away with lending, spending or investing.

By lending, the banker will get interest payments. By investing, he may get rich on profit. By spending, he will put himself in jeopardy: if word gets around that he's spending too much, people may panic and rush to get their cash before it's all gone. There won't be enough in his vaults to pay them all. The game's a bit risky, but the more skillfully the banker plays it, the richer he will become.

At this stage, when the banker lends, spends or invests some of the money he's supposedly storing, he's not actually *creating* money; he's merely putting some of it back into circulation. And 'money' is still gold or silver, or whatever happens to be money at the time.

The second stage towards understanding modern banking is to consider the clay tablet which Remanni-Adad, chariot-driver, got from his bankers. This clay tablet is a claim on silver. Remanni-Adad might keep his tablet in a safe place – or he might try to use it to buy something from someone else – perhaps a new wheel for his chariot. The wheel-seller might happily receive the clay tablet in payment – so long as he is confident that he, rather than Remanni-Adad, can use it to claim silver when he wants to. He becomes the owner of the tablet.

If the wheel-seller uses the tablet to claim silver, the tablet goes back to the bank and is redundant. But if the tablet carries on being used to make payments, passing from hand to hand between different owners, it becomes money in circulation. And it will be money of a new kind: bank credit, i.e. debt owed by a bank.

This highlights the most important *legal* element in the development of banking. If the law only supports the *original* depositor in a claim on the silver, the tablet cannot circulate and become money. But if the law declares it will help whoever currently owns the tablet to claim the silver, the tablet can become money. [5]

When the tablet begins to circulate, there are two kinds of money in circulation: hard cash made of valuable metal, and bank-credit represented by clay tablets (equivalent to today's bank notes). If the money that the tablet represents is still in the bank, the bank has not created any new money, merely replaced gold-and-silver with a tablet that represents it. Chances are, however, the banker has loaned or invested some of the original money, so the banker has actually increased the money supply: he has begun to create new money.

This creation is taken to another level when bankers start creating tablets with nothing to back them – that is, when there has been no deposit of valuable metal. Noticing that their debts are circulating as money, some bankers think: Why not write out a few extra clay tablets (or credit notes) made out to no one in particular? With these new credit notes, the banker can either buy things, or he can rent them out to people who want to borrow money. Looked at objectively, this introduces an element of outright fraud.

There is no 'real money' – silver or gold – to back these new notes, so the banker has created money where there was none before.[6]

---

[5] There is an argument today that credit predates money (see Graeber, 2011) but for credit to become widely negotiable, there must be something owed which has a generally acknowledged value, so the two-tier system must post-date the development of 'money'.

[6] In the words of a banking historian: "The last step in the evolution of the bank-note was the discovery by the [banker] that, as his promises to pay on demand passed from hand to hand as the equivalent of coin supposed to be behind them, so he might, on the faith of his own credit, issue promises to pay on demand that had no foundation of the precious metals as their basis." (Martin, 1892: 127)

There is another, even simpler way in which bank debt becomes money. A bank has many customers. Supposing one customer wants to pay a second customer without using clay tablets or notes. He/she can ask the bank to adjust the numbers in their two accounts, so that the bank owes money to the second customer rather than the first. A few alterations and hey presto! – payment has taken place. Again, debt owed by a bank is acting as money, this time as an 'in-bank' payment or bank transfer.

Numbers in accounts can also be used to create new money with no corresponding gold or silver to back it. The banker can simply write a new number into a customer's account book. A new line of credit, and hey presto! new money has been created for a customer. The banker of course does not give this money away; he or she lends it at interest. This is modern banking in a nutshell.[7]

~ ~

At different times, banks have created money in different multiples of what they hold in assets; sometimes two or three times their holdings, usually about ten times, just before a collapse perhaps seventy or eighty times.[8] A maximum was perhaps reached by Hitler's financiers in Germany, who via 'Mefo-bills' were creating credit up to 12,000 times the value of what they held in assets. (Barkai, 1990: 165).

This is the simple story of bank credit becoming money – and of banks creating money. It seems quite incredible that for hundreds of years, many – but not all! – bankers, economists and historians have denied, ignored, or made little of the simple fact that banks create money.

One banker happy to describe his business honestly was a Venetian banker and senator called Tommaso Contarini. In 1584, he described the simplicity and convenience of a banker transferring what he owes from one customer to another:

> Buyer and seller are satisfied in a moment while the pen moves
> over the page, whereas a day would not be enough to complete the

---

[7] Usher Abbott Payson Usher (20th-century banking historian): "The essential function of a banking system is the creation of credit, whether in the form of the current accounts of depositors, or in the form of notes. The form of credit is less important than the fact of credit creation." (1943: 1)

[8] Bankers tend to keep in step with one another in the multiples of how much credit they create; not conspiratorially, but out of individual self-interest. For this important point see (Phillips, 1931: 74-5).

transaction for a great mass of merchandize by counting a great number of coins. (Cited in Dunbar, 1904: 150)

This passage shows the attraction of bank debt as a form of money. It is convenient and easy, particularly for large payments. It is also safe from robbers, because large amounts of gold don't have to be moved around. But it is not safe from bank failures, or from dishonest bankers absconding with cash.

Tommaso Contarini also described the act of creating credit-money by writing numbers in his account books:

A banker may accommodate his friends without the payment of [real] money, merely by writing a brief entry of credit; and he can satisfy his own desires for fine furniture and jewels by merely writing two lines in his books. (Cited in Dunbar, 1904: 148)

These lines are effectively IOUs. We can imagine Contarini writing a number to say that he owes his furniture-maker a certain amount, and the furniture-maker paying for some wood by telling the banker to owe some of that amount to the wood-merchant instead. Contarini has created money "merely by writing a brief entry of credit".

All these activities emerge very naturally from bankers making use of money deposited with them. The banker, of course, has some anxieties. If his customers all turn up at once to claim cash, he will go bust. He may have to go into hiding to escape his creditors. And another thing: is it *legal* to create claims on silver he doesn't have – on silver that doesn't even exist? He may have his head cut off! This has happened sometimes, for instance in Barcelona in 1360, when the authorities lost patience with bankers absconding with cash and going on the run.[9]

A 17th-century English account (J.R., 1676) says that bankers at least once a year would "sue out a general pardon", to "avoid the penalty of those wholesome Laws made to prevent such frauds, oppressions, contempt of Government, and mischiefs to the Public as they are daily guilty of." Only twenty years later, the English Parliament legalised those 'frauds and oppressions' by getting rid of those 'wholesome laws' – see Chapter Two.

This brings in an important theme in our story: the relationship between bankers and the authorities. This has often been a difficult one.

---

[9] (Usher, 1943: 242). Today, things are a little different: the authorities take money from taxpayers to prop up banks, and bankers are free to enjoy the fruits of their robberies.

Power is jealous of its rivals. When kings and nobles were in charge, they were comfortable with robbery by the sword; they didn't understand robbery by money-creation; they didn't want a 'money-power' growing stronger and taking over.[10] Organised religions were also wary of 'money power'. Judaism, Christianity, Islam and Buddhism all disapproved of lending money at interest (let alone *creating* it at interest), especially within the community.

Returning to the stages by which banking evolved, a few simple developments bring the story up to date. We have seen how, under stress of war, governments began to substitute their own promises-to-pay – their own 'credit' – for gold or silver when it was in short supply, in order to keep the system going. It did this by passing a law to excuse the Bank of England from "honoring its legal promises" (Fetter, 1965: 36) to provide gold and silver on demand – an action typical of special government treatment for finance when the going gets rough. Instead of gold and silver, Bank of England notes were provided and loaned to other banks as 'reserve'. Laws were passed to ensure the public's acceptance of these notes: "The Gold Coin Acts of 1811 and 1812, intended to stop Lord King's attempts to force his tenants to pay their rents in specie *(gold and silver)* in effect made Bank notes *de facto* legal tender." (Ibid: 59)

With the state in on the act, powers that were previously separate – government and finance – became dependent upon each other. A vital go-between evolved: the 'central bank'. The central bank issues the credit of the state and sets the interest rate payable on it. Like the credit of a commercial bank to its customers, this credit is an IOU, a promise-to-pay, this time from the government/central bank to the commercial banks of deposit.[11] Similarly, it pays out nothing but itself – because laws have allowed it to become reserve that doubles up as money.

The tendrils of these interdependent powers extend today into every aspect of social, financial, political and commercial life. We all depend not just on the system, but also on the huge powers it has helped to create.

---

[10] Medieval law put all sorts of impediments in the way of banking operations. Not only was usury – taking interest on loans – forbidden, but "The general attitude of medieval law to the assignment of debts, and the special requirements which transfers had to satisfy in order to be legally valid, made the emergence of fully negotiable paper impossible." (Postan, 1973: 42)

[11] "Bank of England reserves are just an electronic record of the amount owed by the central bank to each individual bank." (Bank of England, 2014)

Now that gold is completely replaced by 'reserve', all money is debt owed by banks – commercial banks and central banks.[12] Today's money consists of IOU's rented out at interest, as opposed to money in permanent circulation such as gold used to be and numbers in bank accounts could be. It is only the act of creation that gives these numbers the quality of being 'debt rented out at interest'. And after the act of creation, bank-money behaves as money should: as property pure and simple, moving between deposits as payments are made, with safeguards to protect it against fraud.

~ ~

It's worth contemplating the nature of 'debt rented out at interest' because it is at the heart of our fraudulent money system. Past commentators have often recognised this fraud, for instance William M. Gouge in 1837 (he speaks of notes – paper money – but the same is true today of deposits):

> ...through the workings of the Banking System, the natural operations of credit are inverted. A bank note is nothing more than an evidence of debt, and does not differ in its essential character from any other simple acknowledgments of debt. But when individuals incur debts which it is known will remain for a time undischarged, they pay interest to those to whom the debt is due. In the case of the banks this is reversed. ... Interest should, if paid to any, be paid to the farmers, mechanics, and other producers and proprietors whose capital is transferred from them to speculators, through the medium of the notes the banks put in circulation. (Gouge, 1837: 9)

All this from simple laws that enable debt to pass between different owners as a thing of value. How these laws were passed will be the subject of the next chapter.

Before banking could reach its modern status, it had one more stage to go. This was deregulation. During the 1990s, the fundamental privileges of banks were extended to other 'depository institutions' such as building societies, and accounting practices were adjusted so that many persons could own a claim on the same asset.

Madness had struck. Brilliant mathematicians were employed to invent new ways in which debt could be created for profit. A fundamental

[12] "...central bank reserves ... are IOUs from the central bank to commercial banks." (Bank of England, 2014)

shift in culture and self-understanding took place. Greed became God. Responsibility went out of the window. 'Bonuses' encouraged reckless lending, and governments committed their taxpayers' money to propping up a system that is utterly unjust.

Here is an illustration of relative change in wages, production and monetary assets (capital) after 'deregulation' in one country (Germany):

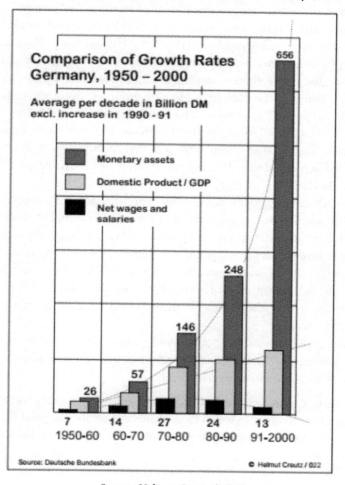

Source: Helmut Creutz (2010)

Sadly, this most important fact in economics – that money is created as debt owed by banks to borrowers and customers, and cancelled when debts are repaid – goes unmentioned by most economists and bankers.[13] Of course, banks also store and transfer money: the literature tends to emphasise those functions, and ignore the function of money-creation.

I have asked many economists and bankers why money-creation by banks is so seldom mentioned, and always I get the same response: it's too difficult for the public and most students to understand.

In fact, it's not so hard to understand. The renowned economist J.K. Galbraith once wrote: "The process by which banks create money is so simple that the mind is repelled" (1989: 29). He also said, "The study of money, above all other fields in economics, is the one in which complexity is used to disguise truth or to evade truth, not to reveal it" (Ibid: 15).

Why, truly, is the fact so seldom mentioned? Another venerable quotation supplies the answer: "The general ignorance (of banking and finance) is not caused by any peculiar difficulty of this branch of political economy, but because those who are best informed are almost all interested in maintaining delusion and error, instead of dispersing both." (Anon., 1841: 81)

I introduce these quotations to show that the statement 'money is debt owed by banks' is not an outrageous and invented claim, but something that has been well known for a long time. Today, the fact is not generally known to those it disadvantages, for obvious reasons. One famous quote on money-creation is attributed to Henry Ford: "It is well enough that people of the nation do not understand our banking and monetary system, for if they did, I believe there would be a revolution before tomorrow morning."

There was not always the same nervousness about popular understanding. In the 1929 *Encyclopedia Britannica* under 'Banking and Credit' there is the following paragraph:

> When a bank lends... two debts are created; the trader who borrows becomes indebted to the bank at a future date, and the bank becomes immediately indebted to the trader. The bank's

---

[13] The Bank of England (2014), for instance, states it clearly: "Bank deposits are simply a record of how much the bank itself owes its customers." And "The reality of how money is created today differs from the description found in some economics textbooks: Rather than banks receiving deposits when households save and then lending them out, bank lending creates deposits."

debt is a means of payment; it is credit money. It is a clear addition
to the amount of the means of payment in the community.[14]

The creation of money by banks has been described – by a banker – as a
magic trick "hardly worthy of a third-rate magician" (Thorne, 1948: 133).
In magic tricks, the simplest manoeuvres are often the best and the easiest
to hide. Audiences are expecting the familiar when actually something
quite different is taking place.

The system is now almost perfected as a form of globalised robbery.
Citizens and customers are mostly ignorant of how the system exploits us:
people carry on using numbers, notes and coins provided by governments
and banks because that's what money is in our contemporary world.

---

[14] 14th edition (1929) & 15th edition (1951). The article was written by Ralph
Hawtrey, an English economist.

CHAPTER TWO

Laws That Make Robbery Legal

A law can be anything from an attempt to establish justice on earth to a device for robbery and murder. Nazi race law was an example of the latter. Most people pay lip service to the idea that laws should be just; but laws are often made to favour the powerful. Laws supporting slavery and laws favouring men over women are two examples (see Oakeshott, 1999).

Today, thousands of lobbyists spend untold amounts of money each year influencing lawmakers on behalf of their (usually corporate) paymasters. Many of the new laws they promote would not be called 'just' by most of us – if we knew about them. But how many voters keep an eye on new laws, to check if they are just?[15] This chapter describes how banks became authorised in law to create money, as part of the age-old practice of ruling classes writing laws to suit themselves.

There is, of course, another way of getting and maintaining wealth and power: sheer violence. Feudal powers depended on violence, and they did not like banking, but over time they too grew to depend on it.

Today, the powers of state and finance have coalesced and are in cahoots with one another. The vital ingredient in this collusion is law, which says that debt can be bought and sold as a commodity. Without such law, bank-credit would not work as money: unless the law says debt can be bought and sold, debt owed by a bank will have no market value.

As outlined in Chapter One, credit is debt lent at interest. When debt can be bought and sold it is called 'negotiable'. To add a little more confusion, it is referred to by other terms too: tradeable debt, transferable debt, commodified debt, assignable debt, circulating credit.

---

[15] F.W. Maitland (1911) predicted that voters would become less attentive to such problems as the franchise grew wider. See 'The Law of Real Property' in *Vol. 1*.

When we make payments to each other, the bank (from a legal point of view) owes money to each of us in turn. Debt owed by a bank is valuable property; it is money: the essential part that law has to play in this, is to support the right of ownership of each and every different person who comes to own the debt.

In other words – as I said before – laws establish that debt can be bought and sold as if it is a commodity, like beef or beans. It is left to regulators to decide who can and cannot become an officially recognised money-creating bank.

Laws allowing money (and other value) to be created as debt are surely the most unjust laws generally in force today, because they allow money to be created in immense amounts for those who already have a great deal, and who wish to use the new money to make even more, not necessarily for the public benefit. These laws are actually very simple, but very few people know about them, and their injustice is not often talked about. People who benefit from them prefer to ignore them – and prefer it if other people don't talk about them either.

'Negotiable debt' means that if someone owes me money, I can sell that person's debt to a third party and the law will help that third party collect. We are all familiar with 'negotiable debt' in one shape or form. We might borrow money off someone we trust – say, student loans from the government (Pells, 2017) – only to find our debt has been sold on to a different organisation, who may be a great deal less scrupulous in their attitudes to collection. We read in newspapers about whole countries being taken to the cleaners by speculators who bought their 'national debts' on the cheap.[16] Most people are repulsed by this kind of thing, so it may come as no surprise to hear that for many centuries buying and selling debt was strongly disapproved of by lawmakers and judges. Debt was regarded as a private agreement between two people, involving real money and/or real goods, not something to be created out of nothing, then bought and sold.

Until laws favour one side or the other – lenders or borrowers – debt is a simple affair. Someone with more lends to someone with less. It's a relationship built on inequality, but the inequality goes both ways. Lenders are usually richer, but they must do without what they are lending until they are paid back. They also take the risk of losing the money they have lent.

---

[16] For instance, Argentina: see (Hudson, 2015b: Ch 25).

When law treats lending and borrowing as a private matter between two people, each party wants the other to prosper. The lender wants to be repaid; the borrower wants time and space to repay. Borrowers and lenders tend to know each other; professional moneylenders cannot prosper without the backing and force of law and the State. As already mentioned, religions tend to reinforce communal ties by forbidding the charging of interest (usury) at least within the community.

As soon as laws began to favour lenders, this community-strengthening factor disappears. The simplest law in favour of lenders commits state violence to force a defaulting borrower to repay. If the borrower can't repay, the state takes some of their possessions and gives them to the lender. A lender may now want a borrower to fail – so he can get his hands on the borrower's possessions. In past centuries – for instance, in ancient Athens before it became democratic – laws would entitle a lender to enslave debtors and their families if they couldn't repay.

This law obviously undermines community ties. It also empowers a new class of professional lenders and acquisitionists, using debt to enrich themselves at others' expense.

A whole other level of exploitation is reached when debt becomes a tradeable commodity. Suddenly value is created out of nothing for the benefit of the lender, who now has an asset (the tradeable debt) in return for what he has lent.

The most widely-used form of tradeable debt is bank-money, which is created by banks as credit – meaning debt from itself. As explained in Chapter One, bank-credit is probably best called 'fake debt' for two reasons. First, interest goes to the one who owes the debt (the bank); and second, the debtor need never pay out anything valuable other than the debt itself – which has become money.

As money, bank-credit is very real: it is used to acquire the possessions of others. And money is just one variety of created debt; its value is small compared to other types of created debt such as derivatives, bonds, finance provided by 'shadow banking' and an ever-increasing variety of mechanisms used by speculators to "get possession of the earnings and savings of many of their frugal and industrious neighbors" (Gouge, 1833: 26). These forms of created debt are known in the trade as 'negotiable debt instruments'. They are claims on assets, created out of nowhere and traded as valuable commodities. The value of 'negotiable debt instruments' at any one time is many times greater than the value of total global production. For example, "Global debt hit an all-time high of $233 trillion in Q3 2017" (IIF, 2018), while global GDP in 2017 amounted to about $80.14 trillion (statista.com) – both figures are US dollars.

The simplest form of tradeable debt is 'bonds'. Bonds are not classified as 'money' because they cannot be used in everyday transactions, but they can be sold for money. The money-value of bonds can itself go up and down, depending upon external factors such as interest rates and credit ratings, so debt itself becomes a commodity for speculation.

The workings of some of these 'negotiable debt instruments' are difficult to describe. Experts disagree on how best to describe them and how they operate. The only certain thing about them is this: they are all created with the intention of gaining possession of other people's goods, and they fulfil this intention.

The right to create debt is supposed to be democratic and egalitarian, but in fact it favours the rich and powerful. Two equal-and-opposite debts can be created out of nothing: you and I, for instance, could agree to owe each other any amount we please – but our debts may be worth little or nothing in the marketplace. If, however, we are powerful and/or wealthy, the debts we create for each other may be valuable to the full amount. In addition, the law licenses certain kinds of behaviour to some institutions – to banks, for instance, in their charters. According to William M. Gouge (1843a), this licensing was never in response to the demands of trade or commerce, but "merely the resort of insolvent governments, scheming individuals, and monopolizing corporations".

A bit of history says a lot about 'negotiable debt': what it does, and who it profits.

Establishing Negotiable Debt

Legal disapproval of 'negotiable debt' was strong in the Middle Ages, when monarchs, military-minded nobles and the Church held the reins of power. Even charging interest (usury) was disapproved of. It took centuries for this resistance to yield.[17]

Why did these feudal powers (and the lawyers who served them) resist the encroachment of negotiable debt? They could see the power of merchants and traders growing stronger and beginning to rival their own.

---

[17] "The development of explicit and unrestricted negotiability covers a period of nearly two centuries" (Usher, 1943: 98). This book contains the classic account of this slow change (pp. 1-107).

In the words of one economic historian, "Each society in which commerce plays a role sooner or later has to face a strong demand to increase the circulation of credit" (Zimmermann, 1996: 59).

'Circulating credit' – another name for negotiable debt – was important for the new power of money and commerce for several reasons: some beneficial, others to feed insatiable appetites for money and power.

When money consisted of heavy metal coin, transferring debt was a much more convenient way of making payments than counting out and transporting gold or silver. It was less vulnerable to robbers, too. And by using 'Bills of Exchange' which re-allocated debts internationally, traders could arrange payments through different bankers in different cities without moving around gold. They could also 'buy now, pay later'. On the other hand, as mentioned above, once debt is negotiable, financial value can be created out of nowhere simply by acknowledging debt. Many writers over the centuries have tried to draw a line indicating where banking stops being a service to society and becomes a form of profiteering or 'unjust enrichment.'[18]

While banking flourished as a kind of semi-legal activity – between consenting adults, so to speak – certain things were obvious to onlookers that are not so obvious today, when bank-money is everywhere like the air we breathe.

For a start, it was obvious that when banks create credit, they create money. Whether the writer approved or disapproved was another matter; but the fact was generally recognised.

Gerard de Malynes wrote disapprovingly of circulating credit in the 17th century: "What is this credit, or what are the payments of the Banks, but almost or rather altogether, imaginary?" (1601). With this imaginary credit, he wrote, banks "do engross the commodities and merchandises of their own country, and of other countries many times also" (1622).

Samuel Lamb (1659), on the other hand, wrote to Oliver Cromwell *approvingly* of circulating credit, and in almost the same terms, recommending the foundation of a National Bank:

> Banks increase the money of a country, allowing it to buy up the commodities of another country and re-sell them at a profit at home or abroad, thereby gaining other benefits of trade.

---

[18] A good example is the centuries-long debate over different versions of the 'real bills doctrine'.

And

> He that hath the greatest trade will have the most money, which
> is of such value that it doth command all worldly things, both in
> war and peace.

Thomas Mun (1571-1641) wrote rather cynically that objections to
banking were mostly "all one matter" and "such froth also, that every Idiot
knows them" (1664: 67).

It was the English Parliament, between the years of 1694 and 1704, that
established the explicit and unrestricted negotiability of debt, giving the
support of the law to credit circulating as money. The story of how this
happened says a lot about who profits from negotiable debt.

Domestic banking had come late to England. It took root during the
build-up to the Civil War (1642-51) when people wanted somewhere safe
to store their gold and other valuables. They left them in the strong boxes
of goldsmiths, respectable English craftsmen and artisans part of whose
business involved storing valuable metal. These men gave depositors
credit notes in return. These credit notes began to be used as money.

As described in Chapter One, by doing this, goldsmiths were not, to
begin with, *creating* money, only substituting circulating credit for stored
cash. But soon they began writing notes where there was no
corresponding cash; these notes were valuable, and goldsmiths either
rented them out or used them to purchase things. Now they were creating
new money and getting very rich off the proceeds.[19] The old landed class
felt threatened. "A new sort of property, which was not known twenty
years ago, is now increased to be almost equal to the *terra firma* of our
island", wrote Henry Bolingbroke (an English political writer and a major
influence on the 'founding fathers' of the United States) some years later
(quoted in Dickinson, 1977: 52).

The notes of these goldsmith-bankers were passing around in
payment; but the law was uncertain. When there was a dispute, no one
knew if the law would help the current owner of a note to claim 'real'
money (gold or silver) from the banker. Some judges ruled in favour of
negotiable 'promissory notes', and some against (see Richards, 1958: 48-
9). This restricted the extent to which notes could become money.

---

[19] An anonymous 17th-century pamphlet (J.R., 1676) tells of an additional,
criminal reason why goldsmiths began to take in gold coin: to take out the good
coin, melt it and sell it for a profit.

The new 'money-power' of bankers and financiers wanted a change to the law so that bank notes (and other forms of credit) could pass freely between different owners and still be legally valid. The Lord Chief Justice of that time (Sir John Holt) was one of those against this development. Holt was a man in advance of his time: he made rulings against slavery and the persecution of witches. His surviving remarks on promissory notes (see Appendix 1) indicate that he thought it undesirable to make a special exception in law on behalf of bankers, which would allow them to evade established rules and principles and make laws to suit themselves.

Principles of Law Overridden

What were these established rules and principles of law? They were fairly elaborate, reflecting the efforts of lawmakers to avoid supporting unjust claims and contracts. Here are a few examples of principles that had to be overridden for credit to work as money (they can be skipped by those with no appetite for legal detail):

First, the rule now known as 'privity' – see (Palmer, 1989) – stated that obligations and rights arising from a contract should only be enforced between the original parties – i.e. not for a third party arriving later on the scene. This would rule against bank notes, which are agreements between a bank and the anonymous and ever-changing 'bearers' of its debts. Bank debts would be 'non-transferable' – like most travel tickets today.

Second, obligations arising from a contract should only be enforced if the person obligated had derived some previous benefit from the contract (rules and doctrines of 'consideration': *'nudum pactum non parit actionem'* or *'ex nudo pacto non oritur actio'*). For a bank, this means it would only have to give cash in exchange for numbers in a deposit account if it had received some sort of benefit from the bearer.[20]

---

[20] "The leading distinctions between simple contracts, and specialty contracts, should be briefly adverted to. The former require a consideration, (that is, some benefit to the promiser or a third person by the act of the promisee, or some charge upon the promisee at the instance of the promiser) to give them legal operation. But a specialty needs in general no consideration to render it effectual. It binds the party, though it be voluntary, and imparts a benefit without any return of advantage." (Chitty, 1834). Sir John Holt objected to bankers' attempts to "turn a piece of paper, which is in law but evidence of a parol contract, into a specialty" (Holdsworth, 1925 and Coquillette, 1988).

Third, you cannot give to someone else what you do not own yourself (*'nemo dat quod non habet'*). For instance, you can't sell Buckingham Palace – unless you already happen to own it. This spelled trouble for negotiability of debt: if a promissory note gives no definite rights of ownership to a previous owner, there is nothing to pass on to a subsequent owner.

Fourth, the 'non-assignability of choses in action'. When the law recognises you have a right to something, but says you need a court order to take possession of it, you cannot transfer that right to someone else. An example would be: if you are owed money, you can't sell the debt for someone else to collect. Because money today represents a debt from banks, for it to work as money, debt must be 'transferable' in law.[21]

Fifth, in ordinary contract law, if a property carries with it obligations and restrictions, they pass with the property to any new owner. For instance, if you buy a stolen picture, it may be seized by the authorities and returned to its original owner. Bank-created money is exempt from this rule. Instead, 'holder in due course' rules apply, so that "a *bonafide* purchaser for value takes the instrument free from the claims and free from most defences of the parties obligated on it".[22] This exemption establishes a bank's credit is pure property, universally tradeable.

The complexity of these rules, and the fact that their histories and meanings are still controversial today, reflects the difficulties that law faces when dealing with claims. A claim asserts the existence of a debt – that something is owed. A claim is an odd kind of property. Most pieces of property are definite and simple: a house, a piece of land or furniture, a vehicle. A claim is different: it often arises from a private contract and it must always involve risk – because a lot might happen between the claim's creation and when it is exercised.

Furthermore, a claim can be on something that only partially exists or does not exist at all (as with bank-credit); on something that might or might not exist (for instance, mineral rights); on something that might exist in the future (for instance, profit on an investment), or on something that exists today but which might not exist tomorrow (for instance, the assets of a debtor teetering on the edge of ruin). It can also be a claim on

---

[21] William Blackstone: "And this property, so vested, may be transferred and assigned from the payee to any other man; contrary to the general rule of the common law, that no chose in action is assignable: which assignment is the life of paper credit." (1765: Book 2, p. 468)

[22] www.bit.ly/TPbr23

something that belongs to someone else – as when people invest in war in exchange for a claim on some of the spoils.[23] On top of all that, there's the question: Is the claim genuine?

Money-Power Wins the Day

The 'money-power' wanted new legislation that would exempt all claims, promissory notes and promises-to-pay from the rules and principles listed above. They won the day. So how did they find themselves in a position to call the tune?

As already mentioned, the English Parliament first passed laws to make debt fully negotiable during the years 1694-1704. Just a few years earlier, in 1688, Parliament had become the supreme power in the land. The new monarchs, William and Mary, had become King and Queen on the understanding that "they would rule in accordance with laws made by Parliament".[24] Parliament consisted then of rich men voted in by other rich men ('20-shilling freeholders'). Among these wealthy men, there was an ongoing power struggle between the old landed gentry and the new 'money-power'.

The two sides came to agreement when they realised that negotiable debt would fund a shared enthusiasm: war. War was looked on kindly by the older war-making (feudal) powers because it justified their supremacy and their existence: seizure by the sword was the origin and basis of their power. War was looked on with enthusiasm by the new 'money-power'

---

[23] This was common practice in the age under discussion. Rulers frequently offered land and assets of prospective conquest in exchange for war finance. For instance, Oliver Cromwell invested in an invasion of Ireland in return for some of the spoils (1640, long before he became absolute ruler of England).

[24] 1688 was the year of the 'glorious' or 'bloodless' revolution when English parliamentarians offered the crown to the Dutchman William of Orange and his wife Mary. The unpopular monarch James II left without putting up much of a fight. "With the accession of William III, Parliament obtained control of public revenue and expenditure and of the defence of the realm. The Exchequer was no longer subservient to the Sovereign; the navy and army were made dependent on the decisions of Parliament. Under such conditions of political stability, schemes for the establishment of a great central joint-stock bank soon came to the forefront of political discussion. ...within six years of the initiation of the rule of Parliament, Montague had launched the Bank of England as a 'Whig finance company'." (Richards, 1958: 211).

because it established new markets and protected existing markets. War is the foundation of empire. By financing war, the new money would benefit both factions of the ruling class.[25]

The first significant law to support negotiable debt consisted of some clauses inserted into an Act of Parliament named the Tonnage Act (1694), whose ostensible purpose was to impose taxes on imports to finance war with France (only later has the Act come to be known as the Bank of England Act).[26] By early 1694, the government's coffers were empty: the Nine Years War with France had drained them. The King was sending his ministers round the coffee-houses of the City of London to borrow money (Temperley, 1908: 267ff). The Treasury was listening to many different schemes, proposed by ambitious speculators, for creating and introducing new money. The proposal for a Bank of England, to provide paper money backed by gold-and-silver on demand, seemed to them the safest. When members were told that a loan from the new Bank would be "the only means of providing money for the navy to take the sea that summer" both sides in Parliament consented to the Act (Ibid: 267-8).

The Bank lent the government £1,200,000 and King William forged off to war, defeating the French at the siege of Namur (1695).

The Bank of England Act (1694) broke new ground in two ways.[27]

First, the government agreed to borrow paper from the new Bank, rather than gold or silver. It hoped that the paper would be accepted by the public as currency. The paper was backed, meaning that members of the public who came to hold paper notes could go to the bank and ask for gold if they wanted to. But the amount of gold made available by investors was very small compared to the number of notes: according to Thorold Rogers, a mere £36,000 in gold compared to £1,750,000 in notes, a ratio of 1:50 or 2%.

Second, the money provided by investors in the bank – paper promises-to-pay and gold – was loaned to the government, so investors in the bank effectively owned debt owed by the government. Shares in the

---

[25] John Cary, a popular writer of the time, wrote: "Credit I take to be that which makes a smaller sum of money pass as far as a greater, and serve all the ends of trade as well, and to give Satisfaction to everyone concerned that he is safe in what he does... It must be such a Credit, as will answer all the occasions both of the Government and also of the Trader." (1696: 24)

[26] The full text of this Act is online at: www.bit.ly/TPbr24

[27] See Kleer (2008): his essay provides a good, short and up-to-date account.

bank were freely bought and sold, so they were in effect a negotiable form of government debt. And the Bank's paper money was a freely negotiable form of private debt, owed by investors in the Bank.

It was obvious to everyone that lending to the government in *paper* meant that the Bank could a) charge a lower rate of interest – paper is cheap - and b) get a much better return on the gold backing the paper. Each pound in gold supported many times its amount in paper notes.

Alternatives were suggested which would have served the country better; but they would have given less opportunity for private gain and state power.[28] Parliament at that time was not a gathering of do-gooders: "Men… no more dreamt of a seat in the House [of Commons] in order to benefit humanity, than a child dreams of a birthday cake that others may eat it", wrote the historian Sir Lewis Namier (1957: 2).

Circulating credit was attractive in different ways for different categories of people. If 'live now, pay later' was the government's motto, 'get rich by creating credit' was the bankers' motto, and 'use new money to make more money' was the motto of speculators.

The Bank of England Act was a beginning and a precedent,[29] but debt was still not generally negotiable.[30] The Act which established *all* promissory notes as negotiable came ten years later: The Promissory Notes Act (1704). The chaotic outbreak of created money and value which resulted from this will be looked at in the next chapter.

As an example of how a few innocent-sounding words can alter the course of human history, I include in Appendix 2 a dusty legal passage from the Promissory Notes Act. It says a lot about the motives behind the Act, as well as being an example of the how legal language is a barrier to general knowledge of what the law is up to. The extract perhaps indicates why it is hardly surprising that most people do not try to understand 'negotiable debt', even though it dominates all our lives: in the form of money, we use it every day, without considering what it is and what it does.

---

[28] For instance, the suggestion made by John Broughton, detailed in Chapter 4.

[29] In the words of Ephraim Lipson it "set a precedent for proposals to accord special privileges to those who lent their money to the State for the prosecution of war". (1937-43, vol. II: 309)

[30] Full negotiability of credit "requires the legal enforcement of transferability or assignment of debts to third parties" (Munro, 1991: 49).

The new law transformed the whole ideology and practice of capitalism. Capitalism was, and still claims to be, a collecting-together of hard-earned 'savings' which are then put to use in a new productive enterprise. Once debt becomes 'negotiable', however, money and other valuable debt can be conjured out of nothing and used to acquire the property and labour of others. Most of this money is used not to initiate productive enterprise, but to speculate and exploit. The devastating results of this transformation are looked at in Chapter Seven.

Over subsequent centuries, laws making debt negotiable were incorporated into legal systems across the world. For example, the American judge Joseph Story wrote: "Most, if not all, commercial nations have annexed certain privileges, benefits, and advantages to Promissory Notes, as they have to Bills of Exchange, in order to promote public confidence in them, and thus to insure their circulation as a medium of pecuniary commercial transactions."(1845: 10)

And so, the country, and then the world, slid from one form of oppression into another. This did not go unnoticed.[31] Early protests against negotiable debt and banking were normally respectful, in the hope that a more just system might be introduced (one example is John Broughton's proposal outlined in the next chapter). But by 1832, hopes of reforming the system were gone. Social reformer John Wade noted sourly that the effect of the system was:

> to replace the feudal aristocracy, from which Europe has suffered
> so much, with a monied aristocracy more base in its origin, more
> revolting in its associations, and more inimical to general freedom
> and enjoyment. (Wade, 1831: 377)

The new laws not only introduced a system of robbery disguised as money. They changed the human landscape even more fundamentally by allocating large and unaccountable powers to government. It was not just banks that found themselves able to create value out of nothing. The laws

---

[31] Historians have tried to estimate the differing proportions over time of cash to bank-credit in the money supply. They have had some difficulty, partly due to the secrecy of banking operations. For instance, historian Rondo Cameron estimated that in 1688 (before the establishment of the Bank of England) hard cash ('specie') was 83.3% and credit was 16.7%. In 1800, he estimated, the proportions were 40% 'specie' and 60% credit; in 1913, they were 11.5% specie and 88.5% credit. Today our money is all created as credit. Cameron 1967 p. 42.

which made it legal for banks to create money also allowed governments to borrow more easily. Lenders no longer had to do without the money lent: they got a valuable piece of paper – a government bond – in return, which they could sell, and which might be more valuable than the money lent.[32] The creation of these bonds was (and is) an addition of wealth to the class of those who own and trade in them.[33] Again, this was obvious to contemporaries, Montesquieu (1689-1755), for instance:

> (National) debt takes the wealth of the state from those who work, and gives it to those who are idle; in other words, it gives the wherewithal to work to people who do not work, and difficulties to people who do work. (1748: Book 22, Ch 17)

A lot of government tax revenue goes to paying interest on the bonds. By 1786, interest on the national debt was absorbing two thirds of all tax revenues (*OEEH*, 2003: 441). (Today, interest rates are kept low because otherwise most Western governments would be in deep trouble: for example, US national debt is over $22 trillion, more than $180,000 dollars for every taxpayer.)[34]. Most taxpayers (then as now) were not literate in the dark arts of creating value out of nothing, so hardly in a position to object. Inequality was rising dramatically, to the extent that whole classes of previously independent workers were driven into penury and debt.[35] However, the general tendency of these new laws and practices was obvious to some people (see Amasa Walker's observations quoted on p. 107).

War could now be easily financed – on government debt. Disgruntled landowners, who had only reluctantly agreed to the passage of the Act in 1704, found themselves paying most of the tax revenues needed to finance the new debts. One of them (Joseph Danvers MP) grumbled that they

---

[32] In the words of Adam Smith, government debt "generally sells in the market for more than was originally paid for it. The merchant or monied man makes money by lending money to government, and instead of diminishing, increases his trading capital." (1776: Book 5, Ch 3).

[33] Without bonds, a substantial portion of the world's wealth would not exist. This added wealth "now exceeds $100 trillion. By contrast, S&P Dow Jones Indices put the value of the global stock market at around $64 trillion." www.bit.ly/TPbr25

[34] Up-to-the-minute figures are available at: https://www.usdebtclock.org/

[35] These dispossessed country folk formed the workforce for the Industrial Revolution. Historians are apt to see some virtue in this.

"bore the greatest share" of the burden of war, being "loaded with many taxes", while the "Men of the City of London" were "enabled to deck their wives in velvet and rich brocades" (quoted in Dickinson, 1993: 28). But – as the saying goes – 'If you can't beat them, join them' and soon both parties were enjoying the bonanza of exercising the supreme power in the land – through Parliament.

Landowners passed private Enclosure Acts – eventually more than 3,000 of them – depriving poor and independent country people of their rights of tenancy and rights in common land in exchange for pittances. These landlord-encroachments were helped by the ease of borrowing newly-created money from banks to pay these pittances; it is far easier to raise capital on the prospect of profit when it can be created out of nothing by a corporate entity, than when it has to be borrowed from a number of different human beings, especially when the project is one that might seem morally repugnant to many.[36]

Both main factions in Parliament were now engaged in dispossessing the poor. While England became the richest country in the world, its poor joined the desperate of the earth. Before social reformers got to work on laws to protect them, conditions for the working poor were compared badly even with the lot of slaves. A visiting slave-owner from Jamaica commented (to an investigating committee in 1832): "I have always thought myself disgraced by being the owner of slaves, but we never in the West Indies thought it possible for any human being to be so cruel as to require a child of nine years old to work twelve and a half hours a day; and that, you acknowledge, is your regular practice." (Quoted in Hammond & Hammond, 1917: 160). The yeomen of the countryside, "once the pride of the country", an "industrious, brave and independent class of men", were "extinct", their descendants "almost the paupers of the nation". (Walker, 1866: 369-70)

How did the ruling classes justify all this? Ruling classes and their philosophers develop convenient moral ideologies declaring them uniquely worthy to rule. An ideology may be political, racist, religious or economic: in this case it is socio-economic, and its development will be looked at in the next chapter.

Attempts have been made over the years to assert that the Act of 1704 was not necessary: that promissory notes emerged from the custom of

---

[36] A parallel is the difficulty William III had in borrowing to go to war before the Bank of England was founded, and the ease after. See Chapter Two of this book.

merchants, and that the custom of merchants is, was, and ever must be an automatic part of law.[37] However, it is a simple fact that the law of 1704, adopted in various guises across the world, put a stop to judges questioning the legality of circulating bank-credit and other forms of 'commodified' debt.

To fight ever-growing oppression from both factions of the ruling political élite, there soon emerged a political movement among working people, starting with trades unions and developing into socialism and communism. Karl Marx armed his followers with a new ideology that would put all credit-creation in the hands of the State. Marx understood very well how credit-creation works.[38] He wanted a monopoly on it for his ideal state. The fifth plank of his Communist Manifesto (1848) reads: "Centralization of credit in the hands of the state, by means of a national bank with state capital and an exclusive monopoly."

The influence of socialism, and fear of rebellion or revolution, certainly restrained some of the abuses of power among the new landed, industrial and trading elites. However, the socialist alternative – a monopoly on money-as-credit in the hands of the state – held dangers of its own. Centralised power in the hand of a single-party state apparatus was hardly likely to be less corrupting than covert powers in the hands of greedy elites.

Two alternatives – socialism and capitalism – were now competing for public support, and both were happy for citizens to be ignorant on the

---

[37] For instance: in 1801, an American court took a vacation so that eminent judges could consider whether an action on a promissory note "could have been supported in England before the statute of Anne (i.e. before the Promissory Notes Act)" (Cranch, 1812: 366ff). The result was a rather strained interpretation of legal history, asserting that the law of merchants was always a part of common law and therefore the statute was unnecessary. This goes against most of the available evidence.

[38] Karl Marx wrote: "With the development of interest-bearing capital and the credit system, all capital seems to double itself, and sometimes treble itself, by the various modes in which the same capital, or perhaps even the same claim on a debt, appears in different forms in different hands. The greater portion of this 'money-capital' is purely fictitious. All the deposits, with the exception of the reserve fund, are merely claims on the banker, which, however, never exist as deposits. To the extent that they serve in clearing-house transactions, they perform the function of capital for the bankers – after the latter have loaned them out. They pay one another their mutual drafts upon the non-existing deposits by balancing their mutual accounts." (1887: Vol III, Ch 29, 337)

subject of money issued as credit. Voters tend to alternate between these two powers, denying both left and right too long a monopoly on power.

Meanwhile in the 'capitalist' world, banking was removed from scrutiny by lawyers, judges, or even elected representatives and given over to regulators charged with keeping the system going. This meant that extraordinary developments, such as the replacement of gold-and-silver with 'reserve' created by the state, occurred without much public debate.

Lawmakers grew unfamiliar with the process of banking. Attempts to rein in the creation of credit by banks, such as the Bank Act of 1844, were undermined by ignorance (in that instance, ignorance of the different guises which bank credit can assume) (Horsefield, 1944).

Judges, too, accommodated the needs of bankers in their judgements. Lord Cottenham's famous remark of 1848 established a principle very favourable to bankers and very disrespectful to the usual laws in respect of safekeeping: "Money, when paid into a bank, ceases altogether to be the money of the customer; it is then the money of the banker."[39]

For the law to support the system, this re-allocation of ownership from customer to bank is necessary. It is vital for the creation of credit. Deposits bring reserves to the bank. For the bank to create claims on those reserves – in other words, credit – it must own them. This is another instance of the law cooperating in the creation of a highly unjust system.

On the other hand, an insightful contribution from another judge, Lord Denning, says a lot about the relationship between banking, law and government (1966):

> Communis error facit jus *(common error makes law)*. ... This applies with especial force to commercial practice. When it has grown up and become established, the courts will overlook suggested defects and support it rather than throw it down. Thus it will enforce commercial credits rather than hold them bad for want of consideration. It is a maxim of English law to give effect to everything which appears to have been established for a considerable course of time, and to presume that what has been done was done of right and not in wrong.[40]

When 'real money' was gold and silver, and credit was numbers on paper (on bank notes or pages in account books) the difference between the two

---

[39] Foley v Hill, 1848.

[40] United Dominions Trust, Ltd. v. Kirkwood, 1966.

was obvious. Now all money is in the form of numbers in ledgers or on paper, supplemented by cheap-as-possible metal coin, and it is not so obvious that all of this represents fake debt.[41]

We can, with hindsight, see a missed opportunity during the evolution of money. Money could perfectly well be created as numbers and paper without being simultaneously negotiable debt: it would then be simple property, circulating more-or-less permanently. Over the years, many suggestions for reform have been put forward; they have gone unheard.[42]

Today, credit-creation is the fountainhead of power, operating beyond public scrutiny, fuelling the powers of plutocracy and government. Public ignorance is a gift to those in power. When money-creation by banks was discussed in the UK Parliament in 2014, most speakers began by admitting they had no idea of how money-creation actually works. The debate (at which I was a spectator) was a dismal, depressing fiasco.

For centuries now, these laws have served power well and humanity badly. Our money-system is the concentrated toxic residue of a primitive structure of exploitation, long past its reform-by date.

---

[41] Historian Bray Hammond puts it like this: "[Banks'] liabilities (debts) constitute the major part of the money supply. The funds they lend originate in the process of lending and disappear in the process of repayment. This creative faculty was far easier to observe a century and a half ago than it is now; for then, the monetary funds that banks provided were commonly in the form of their own circulation notes, handed over the counter to the borrower, and the expansion of the circulating medium was the palpable and visible aspect of the expansion of credit. Everyone recognised that the more banks lent, the more money there was. That is why they were a political issue. [...] Nowadays banks give the borrower deposit credit, not circulating notes, and the result is that their function is less obviously monetary than it used to be, but in magnitude more so." (1957: viii-ix)

[42] In Britain, for instance, *Westminster Review* Vol XLIV October 1873 p 304: "The Power of Issue is, and ought to be, a sovereign right... The power of issue now exercised by the Bank of England, and by the English, Irish, and Scotch banks is a relic of feudalism... The [private] manufacture of coin has been suppressed long ago, but the manufacture of paper money still remains, and the profits of this manufacture are allowed to remain in private hands, the State taking upon itself the manufacture of the only part of the currency upon which there is or can be a loss. It is high time that this state of things ceased, that all rights of issue were gathered into the hands of the State." In the USA, a good example is *The Money Question* (1876) by the industrialist William A. Berkey.

CHAPTER THREE

How Money Works Today: A Quick Summary

This chapter summarises how money works today. For convenience's sake, there will be some repetition and recapitulation of material covered elsewhere.

Our money system is difficult to understand. It is counter-intuitive, so much so that a leading banking historian (Lloyd Mints) described it as a work of the devil.[43]

The system emerged and developed as a method of increasing power in the hands of governments and wealthy individuals. Its power lies in the way it creates, rents out and retires money. It is complicated, expensive to run, and ruinous of many people's lives.

The money-creation aspect of the system is under-emphasised by teachers, journalists and writers of textbooks.[44] These people and most professional economists write as if money merely circulates, is spent and saved. They miss out entirely how it is created for capitalists and speculators, then retired again once it has done its work of (as described by one Founding Father of the USA) "transferring property from the people to capitalists" (Taylor, 1822: 53).

---

[43] In his own words: "It would seem that an evil designer of human affairs had the remarkable prevision to arrange matters so that funds repayable on demand could be made the basis of profitable operations by the depository institutions. It is wholly fortuitous that an income can be earned from the use of such funds, but this being so has resulted in the creation of institutions which have largely taken over control of the stock of money, an essential government function." [1950, p.5]

[44] The Bank of England acknowledges this on their website: "Rather than banks lending out deposits that are placed with them, the act of lending creates deposits - the reverse of the sequence typically described in textbooks." (Bank of England, 2014)

What is 'Money'?

We all know what money is. It is something we own, which can be swapped for other things that are up for sale. Put another way, it is whatever circulates as a way of paying for things.

It is a kind of abstract property. Mine is mine, and yours is yours.

For people who like their truths to be stated with a bit more gravitas, here is an economist saying the same thing:

> So long as, in any community, there is an article which all producers take freely and as a matter of course, in exchange for what they have to sell, instead of looking about, at the time, for the particular things they themselves wish to consume, that article is money, be it white, yellow, or black, hard or soft, animal, vegetable or mineral. There is no other test of money than this. That which does the money-work is the money-thing. (Walker, 1888: Ch.3)

Money has taken many different forms at different times in different societies: it has been shells, salt, gold, tobacco, stones, cows, even bullets. This illustrates the fact that 'money' is an abstract idea which in order to work has to be represented by a definite physical entity which everyone recognises as being 'money'.

The most interesting illustration of money as pure, abstract property represented by something physical is the stone money of the Pacific island of Yap. Stones with holes in them were used as money. Some large stones sank in the sea while being carried from one island to another; but they were still acknowledged as money. It was irrelevant that they were at the bottom of the sea; everyone knew who owned them. The stones were used in exchange for other property – even though they sat far out of reach on the seabed (Gilliland 1975).

The Characteristics of Money Today

Today, as we know, a certain amount of money is notes and coins, but most of it is numbers in bank accounts. We own those numbers: they are OUR property and if someone steals them, we hope they will be in trouble. So, what are those numbers? What kind of 'property' are they?

In our modern world property, protected in law, comes in many different varieties. Some of these varieties have special characteristics marking them out from more straightforward types of property like land or clothes. Intellectual property, for instance, represents things that are real but intangible; mineral rights represent something of uncertain quantity.

Bank-money is another special case, perhaps the most peculiar of all: whether coin, paper or numbers in bank accounts, it represents ownership of debt owed by a bank. All these forms of money signify, in law, how much a bank owes us.[45]

When we make a payment, what happens? Some of what the bank owes to us becomes owed to another person: it is as simple as that. This is what money is today: debt owed by a bank, that passes between people as payment.

The Structure of the Money Supply: 'Reserve' and 'Cash'.

The system depends on having a 'two-tier' structure. This structure evolved from the ancient system of credit-money backed by gold. Our present-day system becomes easier to understand by first understanding the old system of credit-money ('promises-to-pay') backed by gold.

The old system was relatively simple. The banker held gold and wrote out notes saying 'I promise to pay' a certain sum in gold. When these notes were made 'payable to bearer' rather than payable to one specific person – the depositor – they began to circulate as money. Not many people holding these notes demanded actual gold, which is heavy and cumbersome: most customers were happier using promises-to-pay (or transfers between accounts). So – most of the banker's promises-to-pay circulated as money and returned to the bank without the 'promise to pay' ever being fulfilled. As a result, bankers found they could issue a great deal more value in notes than they held in gold. They sold these 'unbacked' notes or loaned them out and became very rich.

In this system, actual gold had two functions. First, it could be supplied on demand to customers who wanted it in exchange for promissory notes; second, when a bank came to owe a lot of money to another bank, it would pay in gold. Because gold was mostly kept at the bank, it was called 'reserve'.

'Reserve' today consists of digits supplied by the central bank. As usual, these digits have other names too (why not add to the confusion!) for instance 'base money' and 'high-powered money'.

---

[45] For instance, in the words of the Bank of England (2014) numbers in bank accounts are "simply a record of how much the bank itself owes its customers".

Now that digits from the central bank have replaced gold, they fulfil the same functions as gold used to. But since digits can't be carried around clinking in the pocket, notes and cheaply produced coins are supplied to represent 'reserve' digits and act as cash in everyday buying and selling.

Banknotes and coins are bought (or borrowed) by commercial banks from government via 'central bank' with 'reserve' digits. They are then supplied to customers, in exchange for some 'deposit-money' digits.

Reserve is an expense for banks and a profit to governments. Managing cash is also an expense for banks but notes and coins are only a small proportion of money in circulation: in England, for instance, 97% of money is debt owed by commercial banks to customers; only 3% is notes and coins.

When banks owed their customers gold, banks (and customers) were more vulnerable: running out of gold meant a serious crisis. Now that banks owe digits, 'reserve' is not so important because the central bank can always create and supply more (at a cost).

Economist Henry C. Simons described banking as "a fantastic collection of enterprises for money-bootlegging, whose sanctimonious respectability and marble solidity conceal a mass of current obligations and a shoestring of equity that would be scandalous in any other type of business" (1948: 198).

Banking is, in plain truth, a system of villainy made legal, protected in law, and protected from public understanding by its complexity and by the convenient reticence of academics, journalists, lawyers and bankers.

How Money is Created Today: A Recapitulation

The way commercial banks create money is quite simple. When a bank lends, it writes down two identical numbers on opposite sides of its balance sheet, signifying two equal-and-opposite debts or IOUs. It creates an IOU *from* itself, which becomes money, and another IOU from the borrower *to* itself. These IOUs can be created out of nothing because they add up to nothing. In other words, banks lend money which does not exist until they lend it. Again, the Bank of England (2014): "Money is a special kind of IOU that is universally trusted".

The borrower's debt to the bank is real enough: interest must be paid on it and it must eventually be paid back. The debt from the bank, as already explained, is a fake. It need pay out nothing; despite the promise-to-pay on a bank-note, you cannot exchange it for gold. But customers do not object, because the law has arranged things so that the debt *itself* is money. The bank pays no interest on what it owes. Interest payments go the other way – to the bank.

This means that for every penny of money in existence, there is a penny of genuine debt from someone to a bank.

A bank will naturally charge a borrower as much as it can get away with for the loan of its debt. In more honest days, as I have already noted, this was called the "magic trick of banking" (Thorne, 1948: 27).

The peculiar status of banks is that they are licensed or 'chartered' by laws and regulations to create valuable promises-to-pay. Other types of money cannot compete, partly because the huge profits made by banks allow them to supply perks for customers – for instance, free-to-use cash machines and no-charge money transfers. Also, because of the nature of the system, they do not charge for money left in storage; on the contrary, they pay interest on long-term deposits because when a customer's money stays in the bank, reserve stays with it. This saves the bank from having to borrow more 'reserve', for which it would otherwise have to pay.

Just as money is created when a bank *makes* a loan, so money also disappears when a loan is repaid (Bank of England, 2014: 7).

Banks are regulated by government agencies to prevent them creating too much money and bringing the system down. Regulators face a hard task, however, because the system is intrinsically productive of booms and busts (see Chapter Seven).

We tend to assume that money is permanent, or at least long-lasting like stone or metal. The malevolent genius of modern money – the quality that makes it an ideal tool for robbery – is twofold. First, it is created and cancelled in a continuous cycle for people who want to make a profit; and second, it is rented out at interest.

As a result, the money supply grows and shrinks in line with the overall need of banks either to lend more, or to call in loans. It is this 'perverse elasticity' of bank-created money which exacerbates booms and busts. "'If the monetary system is to moderate rather than magnify the business cycle, money must be segregated from banking" (Lester, 1939: 292).

Making Money Out of Money

Money can be made from borrowing in a number of different ways. Some of these are:

1. Assets (for instance, houses) can be purchased as speculative investments. If a great deal of newly-created money is being put to work in this way, the price of those assets will go up – a great deal of money chasing a limited stock of houses. Because they are attractive to speculators, prices will go up a great deal faster than the general rate of inflation. In England, for instance, house prices have gone up at least ten times faster than the general rate of inflation since 'deregulation' made it easy to speculate in housing.

2. Existing businesses can be bought, workers squeezed, supply prices minimised, lawmakers influenced and taxes avoided (using a variety of techniques including 'off-shore' tax havens). As a result, profits are increased. The revamped business produces goods and services more cheaply and competitively. According to today's economic values this is desirable, even though it produces a continual drain of money out of communities.

3. Only a small proportion of bank lending goes to new business that may indeed contribute to the general welfare. According to economist John Kay (2015: 1), less than a twentieth of new bank-money is currently devoted to helping new businesses.

All these credit-digits have value because the law, the regulatory system and acceptance by the government support them as 'money'.[46] To repeat: they are a form of property, created and rented out at interest by banks and central banks, then cancelled again when they have done their work.

"Reserves are an IOU from the central bank to commercial banks", says the Bank of England and "there are three main types of money: currency, bank deposits and central bank reserves. Each represents an IOU from one sector of the economy to another. Most money in the modern economy is in the form of bank deposits, which are created by commercial banks themselves." (Bank of England, 2014)

The situation today has become a little more complex, with the widespread use of 'quantitative easing' which supplies reserve to commercial banks at no cost.

---

[46] "…the banks owe their credit to their charters – to special acts of legislation in their favor, and to their notes being receivable in payment of dues to government." (Gouge, 1833: 85)

Quantitative Easing

Most accounts of quantitative easing announce that governments 'create money' to buy assets. This account is disingenuous and confusing because the 'money' they are creating in QE is actually 'reserve'. The government (or central bank) uses the newly-created 'reserve' to buy back national debt – government bonds – from institutions. This new reserve, paid in to a bank, increases the institution's 'deposit' at that bank; but – more significantly – it also increases the reserves of the bank. This increases the bank's ability to make payments to other banks when necessary, and so it also increases the ability of the bank to create and lend new money. Once again, the main beneficiaries will be banks, government and finance.

The public justification of QE is that because banks need a certain proportion of 'reserve' in order to continue creating credit, supplying them with more reserve will enable them to lend more without going bust, thereby increasing the money supply.

With these huge increases in their reserves, banks do indeed lend more. But when the economy is not booming – when businesses are not looking to expand, and their profit margins are shrinking – where can banks look to lend and make a profit? The solution for banks is to lend to speculators in assets such as housing, art, stocks, shares and bonds, which automatically increase in value as money to buy them increases. The cost of borrowing goes down to encourage borrowing which creates new money. Created 'capital' becomes so cheap that hard-earned savings are dwarfed by new money and earn less and less interest themselves.

The value of speculative assets, on the other hand, shoots through the roof and inequality increases. The simplicity of this was recognised from the start, but the process has been continued to keep the system afloat and functioning. These efforts to keep the system afloat have only added another layer to the robbery of poor and productive people on behalf of the established powers.

This and other developments like deposit guarantee schemes (where the government guarantees deposits up to a certain level even if a bank collapses) are a measure of how far our existing powers will go to prop up and even extend the system.

To sum up: the system is two-tier – consistently over 90% bank-credit and less than 10% cash from 'reserve' – and both sets of digits are merely numbers typed into ledgers. Money, which buys produce and labour from across the world, is created out of nothing. This could be an excellent idea if it were done fairly and equitably, in a way that benefits everybody (as outlined in Chapter Nine on Reform). But it is not.

Who Benefits? Who Loses Out?

The government's stake in the system is many-fold. First, money (conjured out of nothing) can be borrowed in large amounts from banks for governments to spend: negotiations take place in private and are not accountable to citizens. Second, the same laws that justify bank-money make it easy for governments to borrow from citizens because lenders get something of equal value ('government bonds') in return for the money they lend. Just as bank-debt can be bought and sold, so too can government debt.[47] Third, governments get a share in the profits of money-creation by providing reserve and cash. Other advantages, mostly concerning increases in power, are listed in the introduction to this book.

The system is a leftover from an unjust past. Whatever justification it may once have had, enabling wars, conquest and robbery, it is now a danger to humanity. The world is a different place today, and our objectives are – officially, at least – not robbery, but peace and justice. But we are still lumbered with this antiquated system of automated robbery.

To finish off this chapter, it is important to remember that bank-money is just one variety of 'negotiable debt'. New varieties are continually being invented, and each new invention sets off a fresh round of robbery supported by law. Derivatives, CDOs, CDSs, repos and 'shadow' banking are some examples. With the introduction of computers and sophisticated mathematics, 'finance' – the creation and destruction of value – has become faster, ever more inventive, and ever more destructive. The system advantages powerful people and disadvantages those who are least likely to understand the process by which they are being cheated.

Those who profit from the system are mostly not very interested in how it works – just as many of us who drive cars have no idea what makes

---

[47] "The security which it (the government) grants to the original creditor, is made transferable to any other creditor; and from the universal confidence in the justice of the state, generally sells in the market for more than was originally paid for it. The merchant or monied man makes money by lending money to government, and instead of diminishing, increases his trading capital." (Smith, 1776: Book 5, Chapter 3)

them go. The obvious fact that private creation of wealth must increase injustice and inequality is strangely easy to lose sight of, especially for those who suspect they may be on the winning side. In addition, the detailed workings of the system are complex and in some of the more arcane areas, horribly difficult to understand.

It is important to remember that this complexity arises from unjust features of the system, not from the nature of money itself: from its reinvention as negotiable debt, from regulations necessary to keep the system from self-destructing, from attempts of banks to evade those regulations, and from complex new inventions which exploit the possibilities of the system to make more and yet more money.

The system is not good for society. Banking historian William M. Gouge's observation from almost two hundred years ago is even truer today: "artificial inequality of wealth adds nothing to the substantial happiness of the rich and detracts much from the happiness of the rest of the community... its tendency is to corrupt one portion of society and debase another." (Gouge 1833 Part I: 138)

CHAPTER FOUR

Early Days

The situation we are in today has evolved over many centuries. Writers on economics had plenty of time and opportunity to comment – and comment they did. Only recently has it become controversial even to notice that banks create money, let alone to discuss the implications.[48] This makes the comments of earlier economists particularly interesting – for their honesty and insights.

This chapter begins with early economists commenting on the increasing power and influence of bank-credit as a form of money. It finishes with a fascinating (and very modern) suggestion from 1707 of how money *should* be created, fairly and realistically for the benefit of all. The idea is similar to many reform proposals being put forward today.

Here are some features of bank-money that writers on economics were reacting to. Some, such as Malynes and Broughton, disapproved, regarding them as unjust; others, such as Samuel Lamb and William Petty viewed them favourably as tending to increase and concentrate power.

- Bankers create more in 'credit' than they have in 'cash'.
- Credit becomes money when it circulates in making payments.
- When bank-credit becomes money, interest siphons money from working and productive people to wealthy and powerful people.
- Bank-credit enhances the ability to make war.

---

[48] Economist Paul Krugman famously said to Bernard Lietaer: "Didn't they warn you about not touching the monetary system? If you insist on talking about it, it will kill you academically." The story is confirmed by Lietaer himself (2013: 36).

For roughly two thousand years, from the days of Aristotle to the end of the Middle Ages, economists did not pretend to be 'scientists'. First and foremost, they were moral philosophers. They wrote about money and power in relation to law and the morality of human wellbeing. Aristotle, for instance, believed that money should be a means of exchange, not allowed to 'breed' more money.[49] Money, he said, is a human invention. We must be careful that it produces good, not evil.

Later, during the Middle Ages, economist/philosophers were employed by the Christian Church, which held a great deal of worldly power. Sword-wielding bishops went into battle, Popes led armies, papal territories grew and shrank: but mostly (and more to the point) the Church's authority relied on its assertion of a moral order. The Church was made up of human beings, so of course it was open to the usual corruptions of greed, hypocrisy and ambition. In some respects its moral precepts were different from those we would live by today, but mostly they were the same and in those days they carried more weight. They were backed by a system of Church Law capable of meting out horrible punishments; and also by the threat of damnation – which for many was a serious consideration.

The Church strongly disapproved of usury: that is, of charging interest on loans. It now seems one of the ironies of history that Christian economists (the 'Scholastics') ignored Jesus's apparent recommendation (in the Parable of the Talents) that money *should* be lent at interest.[50] In keeping with more ancient Greek and Jewish traditions, the Scholastics maintained that charging interest was wrong, full stop.[51]

---

[49] *Politics*, Book I Ch. ix and *Ethics*, Bk V Ch. v.

[50] *The Gospel According to St. Matthew* 25:14-30. Some commentators, e.g. Herzog (1994), argue the contrary: that the Parable was about a bad, not a good master.

[51] Aristotle, *Politics* Book One, Part X; and Plato, *Laws* v. 742. Benjamin Jowett made an interesting comment on the passage in Aristotle: "It has been customary, since Bentham wrote, to denounce Usury Laws on the ground I) that they are ineffectual, or worse, and 2) that they are unjust both to lender and borrower, because they interfere with the natural rate of interest. But in a simple agricultural population where the want of capital is greatly felt, and land is the only security, the usurer becomes a tyrant: hence the detestation of usury. The other and better side of usury, that is to say, the advantage of transferring money at the market rate from those who cannot use it to those who can, was not understood by Aristotle." Jowett (1885) p.34.

Merchants, moneylenders and bankers found ways round these laws of Church and State. They used several arguments: money charged for lending was not interest, it was compensation for the money they *would* have made if they had not lent the original sum (*'lucrum cessans'*), or compensation for risking their capital (*'periculum sortis'*). They also used exchange rates and currency transactions to confuse the authorities.[52] Monarchs and princes ignored the laws.

At this point, it is worth emphasising the differences between money-lending and banking. Money-lending is the straightforward lending of money that already exists. Banking is the lending of money that does not exist until it is lent; banking creates new money in the form of credit (see Chapter One). In medieval times, Jews in Christian countries were permitted to lend money under the protection (and abuse) of monarchs who would habitually, from time to time, rob the moneylenders of their accumulated wealth. Banking, on the other hand, grew out of a practice (the Exchanges) which was forbidden to Jews: it was ring-fenced not only by social and racial prejudice, but also by the compulsory taking of Christian oaths.[53]

Bankers lent a great deal of credit based on very little gold. This made it much cheaper for borrowers – which is one of the reasons why banks were popular among those hoping to profit from the work of others – and more profitable for lenders, because a small amount of gold would support many times its value in credit. In effect, the same gold could be lent several or many times over, depending on how adventurous the banker was. During the late Middle Ages, bankers drove out straightforward money-lenders from the most lucrative markets. Banks were lending credit-money, newly-created for the rich; money-lenders

---

[52] Different authorities notice different evasions, which varied over time and place. There are several interesting essays on the Scholastics in Raymond de Roover (1975).

[53] See *Jews and Judaism in World History* by Howard N. Lupovitch, Ch. 5. The historical remnants of this separation linger today in the different kinds of institution that call themselves 'bank'. Commercial banks (along with their governments) create money in a legally privileged and protected procedure; 'merchant banks' lend it. The name 'merchant bank' is itself a misnomer, assumed by merchant moneylenders at a time when the word 'bank' was more respectable than the word 'moneylender'. Extremists who blame the systemic robbery of banking on 'the Jews' are ignorant as well as malevolent.

were lending pre-existing money, at higher rates of interest and mostly to the poor. The pattern survived until the arrival of 'merchant banks', who are really money-lenders, although they cooperate with commercial banks as well as with many other sources of finance.

Preoccupied with law and ethics, Scholastic economists barely stopped to analyse credit-creation.[54] They concentrated on philosophical and moral reasonings about lending at interest. Under what circumstances is it acceptable to break the fundamental rule that money lent should be returned without increase? St. Thomas Aquinas is a good example.[55] He begins his discussion of the 'Sin of Usury': "To take usury for the lending of money is in itself unjust, because it is a case of selling what is non-existent; and that is manifestly the setting up of an inequality contrary to justice."

As time went on, the Scholastics, caught between the realities of banking and the tyrannical theories of Church doctrine, "were sucked deeper and deeper into a quagmire of contradictions" (de Roover, 1975: 318).

Unlike many, Spanish Scholastic Luis de Molina did at least recognise that bank-credit was a form of money. "Though many transactions are conducted in cash *(i.e. metal coin)*, most are carried out using documents which attest either that the bank owes money to someone or that someone agrees to pay, and the money stays in the bank."[56] But he appears not to have investigated the consequences.[57]

The Venetian banker and Senator Tommaso Contarini was perfectly happy to say in 1584 that a banker effectively creates money "by merely writing two lines in his books".[58] Many economists even today are in

---

[54] "The Doctors, theologians as well as jurists, approached economics from the legal and ethical point of view and proceeded by deduction from a few premises, but paid scant attention to the operation of the economic system." (de Roover, 1975: 357).

[55] See www.bit.ly/TPbr27

[56] From *Tratado sobre los cambios* (1597) quoted in (Huerta De Soto, 2006).

[57] That is, as far as I can tell without having read his thousands of untranslated pages in medieval Latin.

[58] (Holdsworth, 1925: 179). Holdsworth quotes Contarini, as I did earlier and his account is worth repeating: "A promise by a banker of good repute to pay on demand was as good as money and was taken as money. Thus in 1584 Contarini said that a banker could accommodate his friends, without payment of money,

denial of this simple, long-established truth, and insist that bankers are merely intermediaries between savers and borrowers.

During the 15th, 16th and 17th centuries, (male) medieval society diversified from being one composed of 'those who work, those who fight, and those who pray' to a more complex world. The most significant development was the emerging power and influence of a class centred on enterprise, trade and capital. These people became known as 'the money-power'. People outside the Church began writing on economics: humanist philosophers, public administrators, merchants and financiers. Such people, living in the practical worlds of administration and business, were bound to notice that banks were creating a lot of credit on rather few assets.

These practical economists are today known as 'Mercantilists'. Mercantilists disagreed with each other about most things, including the desirability of banking. But they were agreed on one thing: a State should maintain a healthy balance of trade, both to accumulate money for emergencies such as wars, and to avoid running out of coin.[59] They observed that shortages of coin were made worse by bankers hoarding coin as a basis for lending a great deal more in credit.

For the Mercantilists, money-creation by banks was a familiar fact. A sentence written in the 1560s (perhaps by Elizabeth I's diplomat-financier Sir Thomas Gresham) that bankers "do greate feates having credit and yet be nothing worth" was repeated almost word-for-word by the businessman Gerard de Malynes in 1622: bankers "do great feats having credit and yet be nought worth".

Malynes explained that bank-credit rested on very little hard cash. "What is this credit? - or, what are the payments of the Banks, but almost or rather altogether imaginative or figurative?" He went on to explain in detail how payments are made in-bank by transferring money from one account to another (1601: 24).

---

merely by writing a brief entry of credit; and that he could 'satisfy his own desires for fine furniture or jewels by merely writing two lines in his books'. Thus, to use modern terms, the Italian banks had become not only banks of deposit, but also banks of issue."

[59] The rarity and expense of metals used for coin was often (in the 19th century) blamed as partially responsible – or at least, providing an opportunity – for the development of the two-tier system, cash and credit, which now dominates the world.

Malynes called banking the "Canker *(cancer)* of England's Commonwealth" and listed some undesirable results of bank-created credit:

- it fuels wars (Ibid: 26-7)
- it allows bankers to engrosse (amass) commodities and trade for their own benefit, selling the commodities 'second-hand' at a profit (27-8)
- it empowers bankers to manipulate the exchanges for profit and to the general disadvantage (31*ff*)
- it raises prices for poor people by giving power to those who amass produce and control prices, and by creating money out of nothing for those who already have money (28*ff*).

A pro-banking opponent, Thomas Mun, replied in another pamphlet (1664: 67) that Malynes' objections were mostly "all one matter" and "such froth also, that every Idiot knows them". Since anyone with good credit can borrow and do the same, Mun argued, why pick on bankers? We see here the beginning of an argument that might be had today – if the simple facts of banking were publicly and openly acknowledged.[60]

The Mercantilists were publishing their pamphlets just before the birth of modern banking, which dates from when creation of negotiable credit was authorised and supported in law. That birth happened in England during the late 17th and early 18th century, helped on by the fact that conditions in England were different from those on the Continent in several respects. Banking in England was only recently established; Parliament had recently become supreme in the land; and English lawyers were busy adapting and absorbing the 'law of merchants' *(lex mercatoria)* into the native system of common law. This shifting ground in practice and law gave

---

[60] As observed in Chapter One, credit-creation favours those with lots of money. The Bank of England leaves this out of its account: "Banks can create new money because bank deposits are just IOUs of the bank; banks' ability to create IOUs is no different to anyone else in the economy. When the bank makes a loan, the borrower has also created an IOU of their own to the bank. The only difference is that for the reasons discussed earlier, the bank's IOU (the deposit) is widely accepted as a medium of exchange — it is money." (2014)

banking a chance to legally establish itself. And so, it was in England that credit first achieved full negotiability in law.[61]

This development happened it tandem with the expansion of England's power. The 17th century in England was a time of wars: Civil War at home, and wars abroad with the Dutch and the French. For a while (1649-60) England dispensed with kings and queens altogether and found itself under a military dictator: Oliver Cromwell. Parliament sent a humble deputation imploring him to take the kingship, because at least people knew the limits of a king's power: no one knew the limits of 'Lord Protector' Cromwell's (Russell, 1974: 395).

Another 'humble offering' was put to Cromwell by a certain 'Samuel Lamb, merchant': a proposal to set up a national bank. Cromwell's response is not known, but the proposal survives. A national bank, Lamb said, was desirable for the same characteristics that made foreign banks *undesirable:* they could monopolise and sell at a profit; they could create credit out of nothing rather than having to pay for it; they could finance war by means of "imaginary money"; and even, in what seems a very modern touch, they could purchase natural resources abroad thereby "saving our own timber here, until a time of need" (1659: 454). Fast-forward a few hundred years and we see Japan, still heavily-forested, having stripped many Pacific Islands of their trees.

Gerard de Malynes and Samuel Lamb both saw banks as weapons of predation. They differed only in their attitudes: where Malynes was moralistic, Lamb was pragmatic: for national self-defence, what the neighbours have, we must have too. Later (1816) Thomas Jefferson would describe banks as "more dangerous than standing armies". None of these observers would be surprised today to see the peoples of certain Mediterranean countries and many other nations brought to their knees by predatory credit.

The next character in economic history is an almost cartoon-style foretaste of modern power. Sir William Petty is known as the founder of modern statistical economics. Petty was a man of immense energy and imagination, obsessed with mathematical calculations and schemes for the general improvement of humanity. He made an enormous fortune out of what was perhaps the first modern genocide. By Petty's own

---

[61] See (Coquillette, 1988) and John H. Munro (1991) who wrote: England's banking deficiency "may paradoxically have provided the major wellspring for England's precocious contributions to negotiable credit."

calculation, 504,000 people, more than a third of the people of Ireland, "perished and were wasted by sword, plague, famine, hardship and banishment, between the 23rd of October 1641 and the same day 1652" – that is, during Cromwell's war of attrition and depredation in Ireland.[62] Petty was on the spot: his job was to survey the newly-emptied lands and allocate them to Cromwell's soldiers and 'adventurers' – people who had invested in the war to make a profit. Many of these people sold their plots to Petty on the cheap, not wanting to settle in a land far from home where the remaining natives understandably hated them. (Petty, 1799 and Fitzmaurice, 1895)

With Petty, we emerge from economics as a branch of moral philosophy into the economics of the modern world, guided by a completely different set of values: command of resources, maximisation of productivity, and social control. Petty, at the very outset of this development, expressed himself in an unusually direct manner on the new ethics of contempt and exploitation. The labouring class, he said, being "licentious only to eat, or rather to drink," should be restricted in what they could consume. Surplus goods should be put in storehouses rather than wasted in over-feeding the "vile and brutish part of mankind... and so indisposing them to their usual labour" (1799: 240). Independence and freedom were for the few; to be socially managed was for the rest.

"Supernumeraries" – that is, humans not needed in Petty's system of maximised productivity – should be paid to do entirely useless things like building pyramids: "at worst, this would keep their minds to discipline and obedience, and their bodies to a patience of more profitable labours when need shall require it" (Keynes repeats this in slightly different words in Book Three of his 1936 *General Theory*).[63] Maximised productivity should be pursued not to provide plenty for everyone, says Petty, but to increase the wealth and strength of the nation. And once that is achieved, Petty asks himself: "What then should we busy ourselves about? I answer:

---

[62] (Petty, 1799: 312-3). Petty published his estimate to counter a widespread and even more extreme opinion, that 'not one eighth of them (the Irish) remained at the end of the wars.'

[63] 'Pyramid-building, earthquakes, even wars may serve to increase wealth, if the education of our statesmen on the principles of the classical economics stands in the way of anything better.' Keynes (2008), Chapter 10.

in ratiocinations upon the Works and Will of God."[64] One can't help wondering: what sort of God was floating around in Petty's mind?

Petty recognised that banking increased the money supply and recommended it for that reason. In a pamphlet titled *Quantulumcunque* he asks himself: "What remedy is there, if we have too little money? – We must erect a bank, which well computed, doth almost double the effect of our coined money: and we have in England materials for a bank which shall furnish stock enough to drive the trade of the whole Commercial World." His "almost double" was a low estimate, but his prediction that English banking would "drive the trade of the whole commercial world" proved pretty much true. Three hundred years later, a banking historian could write: "By 1914, the great loan-issuing houses could not unjustly claim that it was largely by their efforts that Britain held in fee not only the Gorgeous East, but the greater part of the rest of the world as well." (Thorne, 1948: 31)

Petty made no assessment of how the new money might advantage some and disadvantage others. His preoccupation was: will it be put to productive use? – if so, good. Or will it be frittered away in idle consumption? – if so, bad. This view has come to dominate economic thinking. It is a good example of a moral code built to suit its inventors.

A third possibility of profiting from newly-created money and other forms of negotiable debt, not mentioned by Petty and often ignored since in economic literature, is sheer speculation. This potential would soon show itself in the Mississippi and South Sea Bubbles. These arose from the creation of huge amounts of credit on very few or imaginary assets; the value of the stock grew as more and more speculators piled in, in the hope of making quick profits. Both bubbles burst in 1720.

Meanwhile Petty had died in 1687. Soon after came two developments, both central to subsequent history and both remarked on in Chapter Two: the establishment of the Bank of England in 1694 (originally as a privately-owned bank) and the Promissory Notes Act of 1704.

Clauses establishing the Bank of England were introduced into an Act which was ostensibly setting out new rules for the collecting of taxes on shipping and imports: the Tonnage Act (1694). Clauses 16 onwards of this Act established a privately-owned corporation to create credit-money for use by the government. The Bank of England was to lend the government

---

[64] From 'Verbum Sapienti' (1664) in Petty (1899: v.1, 119).

paper money consisting of claims – promises-to-pay – backed by a 'reserve' of a much smaller amount of gold. The Act also imposed new taxes, which were more than enough to pay the interest on the loan (Broughton, 1705: 6). Shares in the Bank – effectively ownership of public debt – were transferable: they could be bought and sold. In the words of Richard Kleer,

> This loan differed from previous forms of public borrowing in two important respects. Although it was in principle a perpetual loan (no express arrangement was made for repaying the principal), creditors would be able to recover their investment at will simply by selling their shares in the bank (in effect their part of the loan) to someone else. And, for the first time ever in England, the loan was to be paid over to the government in the form of paper currency rather than in gold and/or silver coin as had until then been the custom. (2008: 72)

This was the beginning of modern-style National Debts, raised on the security of the tax-payer and freely negotiable (Munro, 2003: 506). Many people at the time expressed a worry that government would soon become a poodle to the power of finance, and no longer act in the public interest.[65]

The Bank of England came under repeated attacks from rival bankers and political opponents. In 1696 (when coin was scarce because of re-coining) the Bank was almost driven under, in a run organised by its enemies. Then, in 1704, Parliament passed the Promissory Notes Act to settle all disagreement about whether the law should support negotiable debt.

The Promissory Notes Act 1704 opened the most corrupt century in British history.[66] It was also, for better or worse, the foundation of the commercial and military British Empire, financing not just war but also ownership of foreign assets.[67] Today, other countries rival and outdo

---

[65] For instance, John Broughton: "…it can never be the true Interest of any Englishman (Churchman or Dissenter) to have the Legislature (or which is all one, the Command of it) misplaced in the Hands of those, who will ever have a separate Interest from the main Body of the People of England." (1705: 39)

[66] "Never before in English history had so much money passed so quickly through so many hands and, inevitably, some of it stuck as it passed" (Roseveare, 1991: 44). See also Patrick Brantlinger (1996).

[67] For 'war' see (Dickson, 1967); for 'ownership of foreign assets' see (Thorne, 1948: 31) and pp. 97-9 for a simple description of how bank-loans create deposits.

Britain in the race to 'internationalise' their currencies, i.e. use them as value-creating machines for international purchase and predation.

One year later, in 1705, there was a proposal to replace the private Bank of England with a public institution of National Credit, as explained in a remarkable pamphlet: *An Essay Upon the National Credit of England* (1706). It was published anonymously but was probably the work of John Broughton (1674-1720).[68]

This proposal foreshadows many later proposals, for instance the one made by Henry C. Simons more than three centuries later during the Great Depression. It is also similar to proposals put forward by many monetary reform groups today – for instance by Positive Money.

Broughton suggested that the government, not private banks, should introduce money into circulation. It would do this by paying contractors and suppliers with its own notes. The money, being introduced as payment and not by lending, would be permanent, not temporary.[69] Because of this permanence, not much money would have to be created to keep its value constant. The new money would add only a limited amount of power to government, and this power would be accountable because the public would know what it was being spent on. So, democracy would have some say! (Government borrowing, on the other hand, is done in secret, with no objectives declared.) Furthermore, the health of the economy would not be enhanced by arms manufacture and war; on the contrary, they would be a drain on the economy rather than a stimulus to spending (see Chapter 7). The result would be a money supply that is permanent and just.

The value of the notes would be maintained by restraints on the amount issued and be matched by the labour and assets of the English people for whom it is a medium of exchange (this was just before the Act

---

[68] www.bit.ly/TPbr28 – it has also been ascribed to Charles Davenant (1656-1714), but it does not seem to me compatible with his other writings.

[69] "The Proposal, of which this Paper is to give some short and general Account, relates to the Establishing and Extending of a National Credit in England to the great and mutual Benefit both of the Government and People of this Kingdom. (p.1) .... It will certainly be an exact piece of justice, to make the credit of the public beneficial to the public, instead of its being diverted into other methods for the benefit of private persons; and that too, not without danger, as well as loss to the public." (p.20).

of Union, so Britain was not yet a political entity). And the people themselves would reap the benefits of the new money.

Broughton saw economic (monetary) realities in the following terms:

- Because the currency of a nation is used to buy its produce, its value is founded on the wealth (and the integrity) of the nation.[70]

- Because money is a claim on the assets of a nation, issuing it as a loan at interest is a dishonest method of increasing the wealth of the powerful at the expense of other citizens.

- Money, therefore, should be created by being paid out for work done: that is, towards an increase in the wealth and well-being of the nation.[71]

- Money created by the government would save renting money off private bankers and preserve the country from rule by those who have lent it money.

- Notes, being paid out for work and services across the country, would stimulate prosperity across the nation, instead of centralising wealth in London.

- Money created by the Bank in this way, being 'diffused among the people', would promote inclusion, involvement, and commitment to the national prosperity. 'Present methods', on the other hand, involve 'monied societies' – commercial banks – 'engrossing and commanding the whole cash as well as the credit of the kingdom.'

- Broughton suggested that to begin with, notes should be convertible to gold or silver on demand; but later, he speculates on the possibility of a pure paper currency.[72]

---

[70] "Everyone will know who is to answer for it; that is, the Credit of Parliament and the Estates *(people and produce)* of England." (p.13).

[71] "The Benefit of it to the Person or Society credited, is apparent from hence, that it does (for some Time) the Work of Money; during which time, the Owner of that Credit does, in effect, borrow Money without paying Interest for it, and may easily make his Advantages accordingly." (p.2).

[72] Broughton does this by telling a story, in *A Letter to a Member of the Honourable House of Commons* (1705) which ends with the words: "I cannot forbear saying, Happy were England, could this story be told of us!"

- Paper currency, issued by the government via the Bank, could begin to pay off the National Debt, which was already becoming a drain on national resources (pp. 20-21).

- A pure paper currency would maintain its value by being (1) matched by the produce and wealth of the people, (2) acceptable for payment of taxes, and (3) restrained in quantity by Parliament.[73]

- By circulating from the start among traders and customers, notes would stimulate industry and trade directly (in modern parlance 'from the bottom up'): whereas bank-credit creates pools of profit that lie dormant, waiting for the next predatory investment.

Broughton foresaw that objectors to his plan would be, in the main, 'people who have large incomes and make great gains by the present methods.' (Indeed! – And such people were the ruling party, the Whigs!)

Broughton's plan offered complete transparency in how much new paper money is paid out: as a result, it would be more likely to be put to good use. "Instead of being more liable to a misapplication than money, it will in reality be much less... The accounts will be more intelligible and obvious upon inspection, than they seem to be at least in the present methods." How little things have changed!

At this point, it is worth reminding ourselves that there are several different meanings to the word 'credit'. Credit in Latin means 'believes'. Today, the principal meaning of the word 'credit' is 'money in the bank'. But for Broughton and others of his time, the principal meaning of credit was "money that people believe in despite the fact that it's only numbers on bits of paper."

Broughton points out that there is a big difference between his National Credit, which is money created and spent into permanent circulation by the government, and government borrowing. This difference, if not exactly "froth known to any idiot", would have been

---

[73] In Broughton's time, there was a clearer distinction between lawmakers and the executive. Parliament would determine how much should be issued, to prevent the executive from abusing its power. He contrasted this with the "boundless power of bankers" to "extend the credit". Here his proposal differs from that of Henry Simons who proposed an independent authority with the single objective of keeping the value of currency steady, commanding the government in how much money should be issued or withdrawn. In the intervening 250 years, elected legislatures had become less trusted!

easily understood by people in public life. When the government creates money in responsible amounts and spends it into the economy, it increases the general prosperity of the nation. When a government borrows from banks or wealthy people, it creates valuable debt for lenders and commits taxpayers to pay the interest, which is a drain from working people into the pockets of lenders (pp.20-21).

Broughton also points out that the government, by issuing notes, will not be issuing credit 'as a banker does' (i.e. backed by very little) but 'as a merchant does' (backed by a trusted intention to pay) (p.25). Confidence in the credit of merchants rests upon their trustworthiness and solvency; the same would be true of National Credit, which must rest on the honesty, solvency and hard work of 'the Parliament and Estates of England' – 'Estates' meaning people of all ranks and occupations.[74]

National Credit is suitable for use as money, he says, when governments are strong but limited, honest and not 'arbitrary'. His final words are an attempt to flatter the government into agreeing with his scheme. The Government he says, is 'admirably qualified to assist, and equally restrained from oppressing, those under its happy influence.' His flattery did not get him very far. When he predicted that objectors to his scheme would mostly be 'people who have large incomes and make great gains by the present methods,' how right he was! Considering that such people were the ruling power, did he really think his proposal would be accepted? In retrospect, its rejection was inevitable. It was perhaps as great a missed opportunity as England's failure to develop institutions of local democracy.[75]

---

[74] When Maitland addressed this question two hundred years later (from the point of view of creditors of the National Debt) he came up with almost exactly the same answer: "the creditor has nothing to trust but the honesty and solvency of that honest and solvent community of which the King is the head and 'Government' and Parliament are organs." See *The Crown as Corporation*; also *Moral Personality and Legal Personality*.

[75] For Maitland, it was the "great blunder of English law" and a "national misfortune" that the villages and townships of England did not become reservoirs of political independence and power. "It was a grave misfortune that English lawyers thought themselves forbidden to see and nurse into strength the flickering life of the village community." Cambridge University Library Archive Collection, Frederic William Maitland papers MS.Add.6999 'Lecture notes on corporations' (1899), ff. 137-8.

Plans like Broughton's have occasionally been put into operation elsewhere: there will be more on this in the chapter on 'Reform'. Sometimes governments have overdone it and issued too much money: this has happened mostly in times of war, revolution or bad government. For instance, the French revolutionary government issued *assignats* and the American revolutionary government issued Continentals, both to excess, both of which caused massive inflation.[76] Responsible issues, however, made by sober governments in peace time, have been very successful.[77]

How much notice was taken of Broughton's suggestion at the time? His *Essay* was published and re-published, and thirty years later the influential philosopher and economist Bishop Berkeley repeated its propositions in a book that consisted of a series of questions.[78] In a second edition of the book, another fifteen years later, Berkeley omitted the questions. Berkeley wrote, concerning the omission: "It may be Time enough to take again in Hand, when the Public shall seem disposed to make Use of such an Expedient." Perhaps the time is now, to "take in hand" Broughton's proposal – some three hundred years later when the results of our way of creating money are extreme and damaging for all to see – and when voting is not confined to the rich.

Great reforms in society and politics take time. How long, after all, did it take to abolish slavery, to give women and poor people the vote, to abolish the death penalty? Is it really so inconceivable that we might abandon war and make a just money supply?

---

[76] See White (1959) and Berkey (1876: 112-7).

[77] Many examples are detailed in (Berkey, 1876). For instance (p. 43) he quotes Benjamin Franklin addressing the British Board of Trade: "In 1723, Pennsylvania was totally stripped of its gold and silver… The difficulties for want of cash were accordingly very great, the chief part of the trade being carried on by the extremely inconvenient method of barter, when, in 1723, paper money was first made there which gave new life to business, promoted greatly the settlement of new lands, whereby the province has so greatly increased in inhabitants that the export from thence thither [to England] is now more than tenfold what it then was." Further examples can be found in (Lester, 1939).

[78] Berkeley, 1735. Broughton' suggestions are repeated in questions 199-275.

CHAPTER FIVE

Bubbles and Adam Smith

This chapter explores how laws enabling debt to be bought and sold transformed Britain. Suddenly, vast quantities of money and value were being created out of nothing. The effect was dramatic and widely commented on. Some people thoroughly approved, while others saw a new kind of tyranny taking over – a tyranny of fictitious wealth.

Speculators and 'projectors' – people who concocted and promoted (often wild) schemes to make themselves rich – soon realised that when money and other types of value can be created out of nothing, different types of debt can be created and used to raise prices, and therefore value. Assets can be bought with money made from nothing, prices can be talked up, more money can be created to fuel and satisfy demand, and – hey presto! – when the assets are re-sold, sky-high profits are made. The table was laid for an orgy of speculative greed – and the orgy began almost immediately.

"It was as if all the lunatics had escaped from the madhouse at once" commented a Dutch observer (Brantlinger, 1966: 57). Hysteria for speculation took hold of public life. English poets, novelists, and playwrights wrote and argued about the virtues and vices of 'Lady Credit' – and joined in the orgy themselves. Almost the whole of 18th century literature – Daniel Defoe, Jonathan Swift, Alexander Pope, along with many less famous writers – was given over to satirising the new society of speculators and credit-worshippers.[79] Hogarth did the same in art.

The profits of speculation left "honesty with no [de]fence against superior cunning" wrote Jonathan Swift in *Gulliver's Travels*. Speculations in credit "ruin silently... like poison that works at a distance... by the strange and unheard-of engines of interest, discounts, tallies,

---

[79] Nokes (1987) covers this, in fascinating detail.

transfers, debentures, shares, projects, and the devil-and-all of figures and hard names", wrote Daniel Defoe, author of *Robinson Crusoe*.[80]

The risks and downside of this orgy-making soon became apparent. In 1720, sixteen years after the Promissory Notes Act, two massive financial 'bubbles' burst, causing widespread distress: suicides and murders, bank failures, fortunes lost. These were the South Sea Bubble in England and the Mississippi Bubble in France – the latter masterminded by the renegade Scotsman, John Law.

The manufacture of credit-money out of nothing made corruption much easier. A series of plays satirising corruption so enraged the Prime Minister, Robert Walpole, that eventually (in 1737) he shut down all of London's theatres: only three of them were allowed to reopen, subject to heavy censorship.[81] The Prime Minister himself was helping cover up the buying and selling of fake share certificates involving the King's mistress. New levels of corruption were being reached. The poet Alexander Pope's satirical comment was (to 'imp' means to 'maliciously impersonate'):

> Blest paper credit! Last and best supply!
> That lends Corruption lighter wings to fly!
> Gold imp'd by thee can compass hardest things,
> Can pocket States, can fetch or carry Kings! ...
> Pregnant with thousands flits the Scrap unseen,
> And silent sells a King, or buys a Queen.
>
> (Pope in Brantlinger, 1966: 63)

John Law (1671-1729) was one of many colourful characters who flourished in this new *milieu*. A professional gambler, he escaped from an English prison after killing a fellow gambler in a duel. Making his way to France, he charmed his way (and made a fortune) in the gambling salons of Paris. Law was a 'projector' – an inventor of dodgy schemes to benefit humanity and (only incidentally, of course) himself. In the low/high life of Paris, Law found a willing listener and co-conspirator in the Regent and effective ruler of France, Philippe d'Orléans, a man suspected of many crimes including incest with his daughter and the murders of several close relations.

---

[80] See (Nicholson, 1994: 15). Defoe had previously been in favour of credit but in his eyes she was a lady bountiful, whose virtue was easily compromised.

[81] The censorship body set up by Walpole was abolished only in 1966.

Law had no problem recognising that credit is money.[82] If bank-credit could circulate as money, why not claims on other things, like land? In 1700 Law had presented a plan for a 'land bank' to the Parliament of Scotland (known at the time as the 'Parliament of Drunkards'). It was rejected. In France, Law directed the Regent's attention to two other kinds of paper claim: certificates representing government debt, and shares in colonial ventures licensed by the monarch. Why could not this kind of paper invade the money supply, displacing gold and silver?

John Law founded a bank to create credit and at the same time a company speculating in imaginary profit made far away – in North America. With the help of royal decrees, the two men merged the variety of paper claims – government debt, bank-notes and share certificates – into the shares of his Mississippi Company. Shares could be purchased by small payments upfront: by the time full payment was required, the shares had already shot up in value. It was a classic bubble that grew ridiculously big, then popped. New bank-paper was issued in extravagant quantities to pay for the shares. Shares shot up from 500 to 18,000 livres, making huge profits for those who sold before the inevitable crash. The finances of France were plunged into disarray.

Both bubbles – the Mississippi and the South Sea – involved companies with (largely imaginary) foreign projects colluding with government, mixing up the values of government debt and their own share prices, and talking these values sky-high on expectations of profits that were never fulfilled. Share prices went sky-high, encouraging more and more investors – until, inevitably, there was a crash.[83] The herd mentality behind booms-and-busts has been called 'irrational' and 'mad' but vast amounts of money can be made while credit is being created: the trick is to sell before the rest of the herd realises that the bonanza is about to end and makes a stampede for the exit.

A lesson was learnt from these two bubbles – temporarily at least: the engine of credit-creation must be managed with restraint, or it will run amok and shake down the whole edifice of property and power. The

---

[82] For instance: "They (*workmen*) may be brought to work on credit, and that is not practicable, unless the credit have a circulation, so as to supply the workman with necessaries; if that is supposed, then that credit is money and will have the same effects on home and foreign trade." (Law, 1705: 21)

[83] In this way they could be seen as precursors of the 2008 crash, which was also set off by securitisation of debt.

reaction in France was to suppress domestic banking for eighty years, whereas in Britain banking was only restrained.

Once bank-credit was established as a legitimate form of money, the power of Britain in the world began to increase exponentially, helped along by bank-credit supplied for making war. Credit and military success reinforced each other: "The credit of a country depends largely upon its successes, and conversely, its success depends upon its credit", wrote the banker Henry Hope in 1787 (cited in Buist, 1977: 124). Successful wars provided enough real wealth to repay those who lent credit – 'fictitious cash' – many times over.

There was growing admiration (and international envy) for a system that could provide power with such resources. During the 18th century, a new ethic established itself: economists began to speak less of equity and justice, and more of productivity and management. Or, more accurately: economists who talked of equity and justice were increasingly ignored by the establishment in favour of economists who spoke of management, efficiency and productivity.[84]

Internationally, credit was useful for making war, which in turn could create 'spheres of economic influence' where currency created by the home nation could be used to buy up assets.

Domestically, money was created for speculators and exploiters to buy land, businesses and labour: profits were increased mostly by reducing the amount of money going to those doing the work – skimming off as much as could be taken without starving the workforce. Independent workers were dispossessed and thrown into dependence on wealthy employers.[85] A systematic transfer of resources was under way, from productive workers to people engaged in acquisition, management and profit-taking.

All this became known as 'the financial revolution'. The wealth of 'the few' grew at the expense of 'the many' both at home and abroad. A new

---

[84] Economists who continued to speak of justice and equity are still excluded from accepted 'economic wisdom'. This makes their work hard to locate unless the writer is famous for another reason: as a politician (Thomas Jefferson or John Adams); as a banking historian (William Gouge); or as the 'first American economist' (Daniel Raymond). Others, such as Amasa Walker (father not son) and William A. Berkey, one stumbles across only by chance.

[85] This was remarked on particularly by Americans such as Thomas Jefferson and John Taylor who were resisting the establishment of 'English' banking in the USA. See Chapter Six.

ethic was developed to justify the wealth of predators. It declared that inequality is God's reward for a superior type of human, the 'rational and industrious' type. For two centuries, the Christian hymn of choice was "The rich man in his castle / The poor man at his gate / God made them, high or lowly / And ordered their estate."[86]

John Locke, (1632-1704), called by Acton (1877) the "philosopher of government by the gentry", articulated the new ethic. Among civilised people, he asserted, inequality is good, for it is the basis for management by industrious and rational people (1690: Bk. II, Ch V). God gave the Earth "to the use of the industrious and rational", "not to the fancy or covetousness of the quarrelsome and contentious". He praised money *because* it enhances inequality; he buried the fact that the banking system was actually *creating* money for the new ruling class – that in effect, it was creating a new ruling class whose business was making money out of money.

Locke was perhaps the first 'economist' to bury this fact, and his example set the agenda for subsequent mainstream economists. The role of government, Locke said, was to protect property and the *status quo*: "Political power, then, I take to be a right of making laws, with penalties of death, and consequently all less penalties for the regulating and preserving of property" (1690: II, I). At that time, of course, only men with substantial property could vote; so political power was for the few.

The effect, in the words of historian Lord Acton (1877), was that the "divine right of Kings" was replaced by the "divine right of freeholders". Some writers approved, some disapproved. Daniel Defoe wrote: "When therefore I am speaking of the right of the people, I would be understood of the freeholders, for all the other inhabitants live upon sufferance... and have no title to their living in England other than as servants." (1702: 19)

The new ethic of efficiency, productivity, and management favoured large workforces managed on an industrial scale. Just as a disciplined army conquers more effectively than a gathering of individuals, so organised mass labour may produce more – and more cheaply – than individuals operating on their own.[87] The extra profit does not go to the workers, however; it goes to the person with the newly-created money.

---

[86] *'All things bright and beautiful....'*

[87] The classic statement of this is Adam Smith's description of a pin factory, which opens his magnum opus *The Wealth of Nations*.

The new financial system was powered not just by bank-credit, but also by national debt. Adam Smith, Montesquieu and David Hume all noticed that national debt creates assets for the lending class at the expense of productive workers. Montesquieu (1748): "[Public] Debt takes the wealth of the state from those who work, and gives it to those who are idle; in other words, it gives the wherewithal to work to people who do not work, and difficulties to people who do work." Adam Smith (1776): "The merchant or monied man makes money by lending money to government, and instead of diminishing, increases his trading capital." David Hume (1754): "...our national debts furnish merchants with a species of money, that is continually multiplying in their hands, and produces sure gain... the greater part of the public stock being always in the hands of idle people, who live on their revenue, our funds, in that view, give great encouragement to a useless and inactive life."

This initiated a great transfer of land ownership in Britain. Land was bought up by large landowners on created credit, and independent farmers were turned off the land. In this way the 'financial revolution' enhanced inequality and provided a hungry workforce for the 'agricultural' and 'industrial' revolutions which followed. Both needed large, dependent workforces.[88]

National debt, bank-money and war went hand-in-hand from the start of the 'financial revolution'. The English government authorised the Bank of England to create credit on the condition that it would lend to the nation's war machine.[89] National debts grew in the collusion between banks, governments, the 'money-power' and war-making, in support of empire-building and trade.[90] This collusion continues today, with the

---

[88] See, for instance, (Mantoux, 1970).

[89] The foundation of the Bank of England "set a precedent for proposals to accord special privileges to those who lent their money to the State for the prosecution of war" according to historian Ephraim Lipson (1937-43: Vol II, 309).

[90] Various city-states had pioneered this integration of banking and debt; England was the first nation to formally legitimise it and make it ubiquitous and pervasive. Now, three centuries later, we see its full flowering. Not only does the money supply consist of debt which profits the rich at the expense of the productive. National debt also increases the wealth of the rich, creating assets (negotiable debt) for them as a class and charging the productive classes with interest and repayment. As many writers have pointed out, governments could perfectly well create this money rather than borrow it.

added factor that government debt now forms the 'reserve' of commercial banks (this was covered in Chapter Three).

The most interesting economist/philosopher of his age was Adam Smith (1723-90). He is nowadays regarded as the father of modern economics. There is no doubting Smith's concern with moral and ethical behaviour: it is present throughout his work. But when it comes to banking, he appears to be caught in a dilemma, between the old morality of justice and the new morality of management and power.

Smith spent 13 years (1751-63) as professor of moral philosophy at the University of Glasgow. He spent a great deal longer, however, in the pay of the third Duke of Buccleuch, a Scottish landowner and owner of one of Britain's largest landed estates (Bonnyman 2014). Smith entered the Duke's service in 1763 as his tutor (the Duke was then 17 years old) and stayed in the Duke's employ for 27 years. During those years, the Duke was using all the techniques of the new age, including bank-borrowing, to modernise his estate and make it profitable. The Duke was first financially destroyed, and then saved, by successive involvements in two banks: the Bank of Ayr, which was brought down by illicit transfers of money, and the Royal Bank of Scotland, which funded the Duke's recovery.

Smith wrote a great deal on bank-money. He recognised that bank-credit becomes money – and therefore, banks create money.[91] He does not seem to have investigated the effect of this new money on increasing inequality. He also states that "It is not by augmenting the capital of the country, but by rendering a greater part of that capital active and productive than would otherwise be so, that the most judicious operations of banking can increase the industry of the country." (Ibid.)

His message on banking is mixed: confusing if not confused.

His main moral concern was the tendency of banks to collapse, which hurts many. To protect the poor, who are most vulnerable to a bank going bust and its notes becoming worthless, he recommended that banks not

---

[91] "A particular banker lends among his customers his own promissory notes, to the extent, we shall suppose, of a hundred thousand pounds. As those notes serve all the purposes of money, his debtors pay him the same interest as if he had lent them so much money." Therefore, banking operations mean that "twenty thousand pounds in gold and silver perform all the functions which a hundred thousand could otherwise have performed." (1776: II, ii)

be allowed to issue notes of low value.[92] His allegiance to banking seems in part to stem from the new morality of productivity, progress and centralised finance; his most famous passage today is how an organised factory manufactures pins at a far greater rate than mere individuals working on their own.

Smith (Ibid.) noted a great many facts and opinions about banks and banking, for instance:

- Banks increase the wealth of a nation by replacing expensive gold and silver with cheap paper.

- Bank-money makes a nation and its economy less secure.[93]

- Money created by banks may be used in good or bad ways: to fritter on idle consumption, or to increase productive work and capacity.

- Banking is dangerous and should not be a free-for-all activity; it must be regulated.[94]

Smith praised the Bank of Amsterdam for lending no more in credit than it held in gold-and-silver (what we would now call '100% reserve'); but he stopped short of recommending this practice for all banks.

---

[92] "It were better, perhaps, that no bank notes were issued in any part of the kingdom for a smaller sum than five pounds" (Ibid., II, ii). Five pounds was then a large sum of money.

[93] "The commerce and industry of the country, however, it must be acknowledged, though they may be somewhat augmented, cannot be altogether so secure when they are thus, as it were, suspended upon the Daedalian wings of paper money as when they travel about upon the solid ground of gold and silver. Over and above the accidents to which they are exposed from the unskillfulness of the conductors of this paper money, they are liable to several others, from which no prudence or skill of those conductors can guard them." (Ibid.: II.ii.86)

[94] "Those exertions of the natural liberty of a few individuals, which might endanger the security of the whole society, are, and ought to be, restrained by the laws of all governments; of the most free, as well as of the most despotical. The obligation of building party walls, in order to prevent the communication of fire, is a violation of natural liberty, exactly of the same kind with the regulations of the banking trade which are here proposed." (Ibid.) Smith proposes two regulations: no small-denomination bank-notes, and enforced conversion of bank-notes into valuable gold and silver upon demand.

However, it is Smith's omissions that set the stage for subsequent economic 'thinking'. Smith omits certain observations and connections which others had noted before him. He omits the fact that payments made in-bank (from one deposit account to another) are every bit as much 'money' as paper notes are. His omission set a precedent for the next two hundred years, during which most economists and politicians also ignored this simple and basic fact.[95] As a result, two great attempts – in England in 1844, in the US in 1863-4 – to rein in the bad effects of banking were fruitless: banking activity merely switched from paper notes to in-bank payments and cheques. (Ricks, 2016: 230-2)

But Smith's greatest failure was (in retrospect) that he didn't apply his moral observations on money and society to banking.

Smith observed that a working economy feeds money to "three different orders of people; to those who live by rent, to those who live by wages, and to those who live by profit". "Those who live by profit" have "not the same connection with the general interest of the society" as owners and wage-earners (1776: Bk 1, Ch 11). Individuals of the first two orders desire prosperity for all, he wrote, because it is in their own interests that everyone should prosper. Only the third order – those who live by profit – get more by taking everything for themselves and leaving everyone else with nothing.[96]

Smith never underestimates stupidity and malevolence in the ruling class. "All for ourselves, and nothing for other people, seems, in every age of the world, to have been the vile maxim of the masters of mankind." (Ibid.: III, iv). But he did not want profit-takers to displace the old order: "The violence and injustice of the rulers of mankind is an ancient evil, for which, I am afraid, the nature of human affairs can scarce admit of a remedy. But the mean rapacity, the monopolising spirit of merchants and manufacturers... may very easily be prevented from disturbing the tranquility of anybody but themselves" (Ibid.: IV, iii).

But in this connection, Smith failed to examine the consequences of banks creating money when they lend. Banks lend on one single

---

[95] It is common today to assert that this was only noticed early in the twentieth century. In fact, see Chapters 1 and 2 of this book for a great deal of evidence to the contrary.

[96] Profit-takers are not subject to Smith's famous 'invisible hand' (which makes the butcher supply good meat because his customers will come again) because they have no connection with those they profit from.

consideration: whether both parties will make a profit. In other words, banks favour the order of profit-seekers "whose interest" (in Smith's own words) "is never exactly the same with that of the public, who have generally an interest to deceive and even to oppress the public, and who accordingly have, upon many occasions, both deceived and oppressed it." Banks also annul money once that profit is taken, so that more can be created. They therefore continually supply new money to those who want to rob and oppress. This was not perhaps so clear in Smith's day as it is in our own. But his failure, and his immense influence on subsequent economic thinking, have licensed subsequent economists to ignore this too.

Smith came down morally harder on public debt than he did on banking. "The interest *(on public debt)*," he wrote, "is paid by industrious people, and given to support idle people who are employed in gathering it. Thus industry is taxed to support idleness." (1896: 210)

When Smith makes his final moral assessment of whether banks are a 'good thing' he switches to the new morality of efficiency, in which productivity is a good thing – full stop. After long (and somewhat inconsistent) argument, he concludes that banking (when judiciously conducted) is on balance a good thing, because the operations of banking turn dead stock into productive capital.[97]

The Wealth of Nations is a 'great' book. It set the stage for two and a half centuries of empire-building and became the economic Bible of the new ruling class, a place it still holds today. But sadly, its neglect of the effects of negotiable debt set a precedent for mainstream economics which has been followed ever since. This neglect has permeated and distorted every area of economics. "Since Adam Smith, the development of economics has been one long chain of making rules, refuting them, qualifying them, forgetting them" (Tilden, 1935).

After Smith, economics became less a scientific endeavour to understand, more a series of efforts at shoring up the great and overweening powers which succeed one another, each hoping to use the

---

[97] 'the judicious operations of banking enable him *(a trader)* to convert this dead stock *(cash)* into active and productive stock; into materials to work upon, into tools to work with, and into provisions and subsistence to work for; into stock which produces something both to himself and to his country. (1776: II, ii)

power of created credit for its own ends: predatory capitalism, socialism, communism, fascism and now the 'enterprise state'.[98]

Since Smith, it is mostly outsiders who have written of injustice in money-creation. Their insights do not form part of what is taught as 'economics' across the generations. Instead, their ideas drift like icebergs in fog, slowly melting unnoticed.

The idea that economics should serve justice rather than power resurfaced with early American economists: John Taylor (1753-1824), Daniel Raymond (1786-1849), William M. Gouge (1796-1863) and Amasa Walker (1799-1875). The story is intimately bound up with the disappointments of people (like founding fathers Thomas Jefferson and John Adams) who hoped the United States would eventually become a New World of justice, equity and peace. The story of how 'English banking' turned it instead into something quite different will be the subject of the next chapter.

---

[98] For the 'enterprise state' in relation to freedom and civil society, see Michael Oakeshott, *On Human Conduct*; also, with specific reference to economics, his essay *The Political Economy of Freedom*.

CHAPTER SIX

America, Won and Lost

After the United States gained its independence, it became powerful in the world in two very different ways: as an idea, and as a reality.

'America the idea' is a land of freedom and democracy, equality and opportunity, promoting these aspirations and values across the world.

'America the reality' is an international power built on genocide and slavery. Today, a carefully managed monetary system allots wealth to those who do no productive work. In the wider world, America destabilises popular governments, promotes tyrannies, creates dollars to purchase foreign resources for corporate exploitation and sponsors foreign wars that establish new bases of military and financial power.

For a long time 'American the idea' successfully camouflaged the activities of 'America the reality'. Today the camouflage is wearing very thin. The development of 'America the reality' occurred as the powers of money and corporate industry won out over the idealism and the good intentions of many of its 'founding fathers'[99] – and of countless others. Central to this development was the adoption of British banking as a way of creating money.

The adoption of British banking by America has an interesting history. After independence, the American elite opted for the method favoured by their old colonial masters and rejected homegrown approaches to money-creation, some of which had been both just and efficient (see below).

The new elite liked British banking for the same reason it was loved by the British parliament – because it favoured government power and private wealth. The collusion of finance and government power, via

---

[99] John Adams put his hopes thus: "I always consider the settlement of America as the opening of a grand scheme and design in Providence for the emancipation and illumination of the slavish part of mankind all over the Earth."

circulating credit, is a very resilient form of concentrated power, because although everyone can see the bad effects, few people understand how it works. Governments across the world have since adopted the method for the same reasons: to augment their own power, and to make it easy for their supporters to increase their own wealth.

Money Creation in Colonial Times

During colonial times, there were no private banks in America: the first private commercial bank, the Bank of North America, was chartered in 1781 during the War of Independence (1775–1783). Nor were there any mines for gold or silver. As a result, there was a chronic shortage of metal money, both for domestic use and for buying imports from abroad.

Out of need, some colonial governments began to create their own paper money. When they created money responsibly – that is, to help their citizens, rather than to increase the powers of government – the result was prosperity.

Responsible money creation means two things: first, not creating too much (which causes inflation and devalues money); and secondly, creating it as property, not as debt rented out at interest. In these circumstances, the two-tier system of reserve and promises-to-pay (credit) is avoided completely. New money is spent by the government into the economy for services done and is, from the start, circulating property. Such notes were guaranteed by being convertible into a certain amount of gold.

When money was created responsibly in this manner, prosperity would arrive almost overnight. "When Maryland first issued paper money in 1733, most of it was given away—a certain sum to each inhabitant over 15 years of age." The result: "Hitherto, nearly all the people in the province had been engaged in the raising of tobacco... But now, wheat was raised, roads were cleared, bridges were built, towns sprang up, and facilities of social and commercial intercourse were thereby greatly increased."[100] Benjamin Franklin made similar observations about the effects of paper money in Pennsylvania.

---

[100] (Lester 1939, pp 142-151). He quotes from Gould, *Money and Transportation in Maryland* 1720-1765 (1915) and Mereness, *Maryland as a Proprietary Province* (1901). See also www.bit.ly/TPbr49

These and other successful experiments in the American colonies proved, in the words of William Hixson (2005: 91-2), that "private banks, as creators of banknotes or bank credit, are totally unnecessary for economic growth and prosperity."

In 1751 and 1764, the British Parliament put restraints on colonial governments engaged in printing 'legal tender' paper money. Supposedly, this was for the good of the colonies, but Benjamin Franklin (1767) objected: "Paper money does not have the ruinous nature ascribed to it. Far from being ruined by it, the colonies that have made use of paper money have been and are all in a thriving condition." The motives of Parliament were not altruistic, but an attempt to keep power in British hands.

The Constitutional Convention

Soon after the rebels won their independence, delegates from the new United States assembled to decide on a new Constitution (1787). Right from the start, the question 'Who should create the money supply?' was a subject of contention.

During the war of Independence, the rebels had printed paper money called 'Continentals'. In the heat and needs of war, they had printed irresponsibly and far too much. The notes had become almost worthless.[101] This added a chaotic element to the difficulties of state governments and individuals when settling payments and debts.[102] And it undermined the idea that paper money was a good thing.

But another factor was at play. British-style private banking had arrived in 1781, six years before the Constitutional Convention. It was already making some people very rich. Some delegates were invested in banks and were in favour of private banks creating money.[103] Bray Hammond, our most authoritative historian of banking during that period, writes: "Within the convention, banks had more friends than

---

[101] George Washington wrote in 1779 "a wagon load of money will scarcely purchase a wagon load of provisions." www.bit.ly/TPbr29

[102] "It was the damage of legal tender laws to interstate relations, rather than the possibility of bank notes or the memory of Continentals, that resulted in the Constitutional prohibition of state paper money." (Schweitzer, 1989)

[103] "Seven delegates at least were stockholders in the Bank of North America" (Hammond, 1957: 104).

enemies, but outside, it was the other way around" (1957: 105). Surely, an early sign of representatives representing their own interests above those of the people!

Passions were strong on both sides – or rather on all sides, for there were several areas of disagreement. As well as 'Should private banks be allowed to create money?' there were questions such as: 'Should the federal government create and manage money?' and 'Should each State be allowed to work out its own monetary arrangements?' and 'Should *no one* be allowed to create money out of (almost) nothing: should money consist only of precious metals, whose value as coin stays as close as possible to the market value of its metals?'. Delegates left most of these money-questions open for the future to decide. The only definite pronouncement was that individual state governments should *not* be allowed to print paper money.[104]

With that pronouncement, the ability of individual State governments to issue paper money, responsibly or otherwise, was ended. "State paper money had formed an integral part of the money supply of the colonies through the 1700s; the Constitution prohibited not merely additions to the money supply, but an entire category of money." (Schweitzer, 1989)

There was even stronger feeling against the *federal* government creating the money supply: it would be giving too much power to central government. The division of power between state and federal government was the most burning issue at the Convention. Delegates recognised, however, that in emergencies such as war, federal creation of money might be a necessity. As a result, nothing definite was stated: again, it was left for the future to decide.

And on private banking, the Constitution was silent. "There is nothing in the Constitution about banks and banking," writes Bray Hammond, "though there might well have been, for the subject was already of both economic and political importance when the Constitution was being written." He suggests the reason: "in all likelihood, it was because the subject was too touchy". As a result, banks were left to create the money supply. The number of banks grew steadily: "The records indicate that in 1801 there were 31 banks, in 1829 there were 329, and in 1837 there were 788" (1957: 103). Commercial banks were using government debt, as well

---

[104] "With respect to paper money [the Constitution] forbade the states to issue it but omitted to say what the federal government might do" (Hammond, 1957: 92)

as gold and silver, to back their notes, so private banks were a source of borrowing and power for governments. (Hammond, 1947: 7)

With state and federal governments constitutionally forbidden to create paper money, the field was laid open for private banks to get to work, printing and lending notes, writing in deposits, and generally creating money as debt and lending it. As already mentioned, this involves the bank creating two equal debts out of nothing, one of which is legally enabled as money; as a result, interest payments go one way – to the bank. Governments both federal and state were immediately able to borrow large amounts, charging the interest on the debt to citizens (via taxation), and to use the money for their own purposes, good or bad, without consulting their citizens.[105]

Many fundamental questions about money which had been discussed in colonial days were not discussed at all at the Convention; such as:

- Should new money be distributed equitably, or should it profit just a few?

- If money is to be created as debt *from* an institution, is it right that interest should be charged?

- Should paper money be 'backed' by some obviously valuable commodity such as gold or land?

- Should money be permanent or short-lived?

- Who should decide how much money to create at any one time?

- What aims and objectives should govern decision-making about money?[106]

These questions never surfaced; the overriding concern at the Convention was the conflict between state and federal rights and powers. Once the constitution was ratified, is became a semi-divine institution only open to questioning at the highest levels.

As well as conflicting interests and emotions, ignorance affected the debate over banks and bank-money. Although it was obvious that when banks printed notes they were creating new money, other basic facts were understood only by a few. Alexander Hamilton seems to have been one of

---

[105] The usual enabling act for a state bank involved lending the state money in return for state debt.

[106] Benjamin Franklin's writings (see bibliography) on paper money are a good example of concern with these questions. See also (Grubb, 2007).

the few to understand, for instance, that payments made between bank deposits are also a form of money. He also understood that banks create money when they lend – and extinguish money when a loan is repaid. His explanation (1790) of how money works is brilliant:

> Every loan which a bank makes is, in its first shape, a credit given to the borrower in its books, the amount of which it stands ready to pay, either in its own notes or in gold or silver, at his option. But, in a great number of cases, no actual payment is made in either. The borrower frequently, by a check or order, transfers his credit to some other person, to whom he has a payment to make; who, in his turn, is as often content with a similar credit, because he is satisfied that he can, whenever he pleases, either convert it into cash *(gold and/or silver)* or pass it to some other hand, as an equivalent for it. And in this manner the credit keeps circulating, performing, in every stage, the office of money, till it is extinguished by a discount with some person who has a payment to make to the bank to an equal or greater amount. (cited in Dunbar, 1904: 121)

Hamilton, however, was in favour of banking and most things British. He advocated strong power for federal government and was contemptuous of democracy: in his very last letter he wrote, "our real Disease... is Democracy, the poison of which by a subdivision will only be the more concentrated in each part, and consequently the more virulent."[107]

For George Washington, strong central power was desirable to prevent the new nation from tearing itself apart. He trusted his Secretary of the Treasury – none other than Alexander Hamilton – with economic policy. Hamilton designed a charter for a federal bank, the first Bank of the United States, to finance government expenditure. Washington signed the bill. Again, in the words of Bray Hammond: "Alexander Hamilton prepared America for an imperial future of wealth and power, mechanized beyond the handicraft stage of his day and amply provided with credit to that end." (1957: 121)

Washington, however, deplored the empire-building potential in centralised power. The prospect of America competing for empire on the international stage was a vision that disturbed him greatly: he warned against it in his Farewell Address (1796).

---

[107] To T. Sedgwick Esqr. New York July 10, 1804.

By creating money out of nothing, banks were able to lend money cheaply in large amounts, and to provide their clients with free payment services. For those who were already wealthy, it was a win-win situation. Wealthy elites of both political parties – at the time, 'Republican' and 'Federalist' – competed shamelessly to found banks that would support partisan business. (Hammond, 1957: Ch 6)

During the next hundred years, arguments pro- and anti-banking focused on paper vs metal money. The subject of payments between bank deposits – another form of money requiring no actual pay-out of gold or silver – was largely ignored. Paper money is obviously created out of very little – and worth a lot. Deposits, on the other hand, are confusing: they can be created by a genuine deposit of silver, gold or already existing bank numbers; or they can be created when a loan is made, by the bank merely writing numbers into an account and loaning out these valuable numbers -which are money, because the law enables them to be money.[108]

This focus on paper-money, among public and politicians alike, misled efforts at reforming money-creation. Even the most concerted and popular attempts to reform banking foundered. Often, they even contributed to their own failure, as will be seen later in this chapter.

Jefferson, Adams, Taylor

The strongest opponents of 'English' banking practices among the Founding Fathers – John Adams and Thomas Jefferson, second and third Presidents of the United States – were abroad in France and England while the Constitution was being discussed.[109] Although rivals in politics, they agreed on the subject of banking. Having spent many years in Europe, they were familiar with its results. A mutual friend, John Taylor of Caroline, Virginia, also objected to private money-creation.

Thomas Jefferson wrote, in a letter to John Taylor:

---

[108] Bray Hammond (1957: 139) writes that in the 18th century it was common knowledge that banks create deposits; this knowledge was lost in the 19th century. Occasionally, an academic would write to remind everyone of this fact, as for instance Charles Franklin Dunbar (1887).

[109] Benjamin Franklin died in 1790, having given little indication of what he thought of private commercial banks creating money beyond buying a few shares in the Bank of North America (his grandson was printing their notes).

The system of banking we have both equally and ever reprobated. I contemplate it as a blot left in all our constitutions, which, if not covered, will end in their destruction, which is already hit by the gamblers in corruption, and is sweeping away in its progress the fortunes and morals of our citizens… I sincerely believe, with you, that banking establishments are more dangerous than standing armies; and that the principle of spending money to be paid by posterity, under the name of funding, is but swindling futurity on a large scale. (28 May, 1816)

By funding, Jefferson meant government borrowing: charging the interest to taxpayers and giving the lenders valuable bonds – debt certificates – that they could sell. By 'swindling futurity' he meant loading debt onto subsequent generations, while creating money for use in the present. (As already mentioned, today's US national debt is over $22 trillion, more than $180,000 dollars for every taxpayer.)[110]

Jefferson complained in a letter to William B. Giles (Dec 1825) that government in the USA was becoming "an aristocracy, founded on banking institutions and moneyed incorporations under the guise and cloak of their favored branches of manufactures, commerce and navigation, riding and ruling over the plundered ploughman and beggared yeomanry." John Adams wrote, again to John Taylor:

I have never had but one opinion concerning banking… and that opinion has uniformly been that the banks have done more injury to the religion, morality, tranquility, prosperity, and even wealth of the nation, than they can have done or ever will do good. (12 March, 1819)[111]

Their friend John Taylor wrote a great deal about money. Unlike Adams and Jefferson, he had no great political ambition. He never became President, and today his name is largely lost in obscurity. Nevertheless, his writings expressed the ideas and ideals of many at the time.[112]

---

[110] Up-to-the-minute figures are available at: https://www.usdebtclock.org/

[111] Despite this, the number of banks tripled during Adams' and Jefferson's presidencies.

[112] From Wikipedia: "Sheldon and Hill (*The Liberal Republicanism of John Taylor of Caroline*, 2008) locate Taylor at the intersection of republicanism and classical liberalism. They see his position as a 'combination of a concern with Lockean natural rights, freedom, and limited government along with a classical

A currency of credit, Taylor wrote,

> possesses an unlimited power of enslaving nations, if slavery consists in binding a great number to labour for a few. Employed, not for the useful purpose of exchanging, but for the fraudulent one of transferring property, currency is converted into a thief and a traitor, and begets, like an abuse of many other good things, misery instead of happiness. (1814: 292)

Banking, he wrote, was "a machine for transferring property from the people to capitalists". The machine "is worked by fictitious capital, but the machine itself is no fiction" (1822). He noted the following points about banking and bank-created money:

- Bank-money "robs all useful occupations of a great portion of their labour" by taking profits from workers and giving them to those who contribute nothing (1820: 209). It is fictitious debt, "for which the community pays something for nothing" (1814: 16-18).

- Banking is not a product of nature or law, but of "legal abuse" (1822: 236).

- Banking puts working people in servitude to people who contribute nothing (1814: 354).

- Banking makes a mockery of democracy, for it concentrates wealth and wealth is power.[113]

- The banking system takes money out of equitable circulation and concentrates it in fewer and fewer hands. As a result, prosperity suffers (1822: 39-40).

- Ordinary people are deluded into thinking that banking is the source of prosperity, when in fact it profits only a few and impoverishes everyone else (1794: 19).

- Banking allocates money in a way that corrupts capitalism: "capital is only useful and reproductive, when it is obtained by fair and

---

interest in strong citizen participation in rule to prevent concentrated power and wealth, political corruption, and financial manipulation' (p. 224)."

[113] "Wealth, like suffrage, must be considerably distributed to sustain a democratick republic; and hence, whatever draws a considerable proportion of either into a few hands, will destroy it. As power follows wealth, the majority must have wealth or lose power." (1814: 274-5).

honest industry… Whenever it is created by legal coercions, the productiveness of the common stock of capital is diminished." (1820: 234)

Taylor called the collusion of government and created capital a "tyranny of fraud". Looking at England, at that time the most successful commercial nation in the world, he saw poverty and destitution plaguing the masses, and immense wealth gained by just a few. Wealth was being diverted away from working people "into the pockets of the government, and of the exclusively privileged allies it has created." Banking and government debt, he wrote, are the basis of a new "paper feudal system" (1814: 290ff).

As the 19th century progressed, arguments over the powers of banks shifted from 'Should they exist at all?' to 'Who should control them?'. Banks were now established, and only a few voices in the wilderness advocated returning to another and very different kind of money – the kind created by State governments not as debt, but as permanently circulating money (Lester, 1939: 142-151). Banks were well entrenched; not because bankers were pulling the strings, but because everyone with power and wealth, including state and federal governments, appreciated the banks' ability to supply them with money cheaply and in large amounts.[114]

Furthermore, a new spirit had taken hold of the nation. Bray Hammond quotes a wise and distinguished old man (Albert Gallatin, 1761-1849) who had seen it all:

> The energy of this nation is not to be controlled; it is at present exclusively applied to the acquisition of wealth and to improvements of stupendous magnitude. Whatever has that tendency, and of course an immoderate expansion of credit, receives favor…. But it seems to me as if general demoralization was the consequence; I doubt whether general happiness is increased; and I would have preferred a gradual, slower, and more secure progress.

Hammond (1957: 279-85) describes a pervasive and distressing pattern: initial hard-working pioneers developing the land were bankrupted by loans, their properties taken over by speculators. The expense of stock and

---

[114] Bray Hammond (1936: 191) again: "What was wanted was 'money,' and the way to get it was to have 'banks.'"

equipment was met with loans; when times were good, everyone prospered and interest payments were met; when times were bad, loans were called in.

The spirit of 'enterprise' – getting rich on borrowed money – became the functioning god of America. 'Democratisation' meant making credit available to everyone who wanted it, giving an advantage to individuals with a lust for pure money as against those who want to give to society as much as they get.

Jackson, Raymond, Gouge

The most public and dramatic episode in U.S. history in respect of resistance to banking was President Andrew Jackson's attempt to destroy banking altogether. Jackson had two bugbears: central government (too strong) and the evils of banking. He had two terms in office as President: 1829-33 and 1833-37.

Banking in America, to a greater extent than in Europe, consisted mostly of creating (and lending) paper money. It was plainly obvious that some people were benefiting from this created value at the expense of others.[115] The process is so obviously unfair, a moral had to be invented to justify it. This moral amounted to: credit-creation is a golden highway to wealth and it should be 'democratically' open to all. Whether someone gets rich depends upon the strength of their enterprising spirit.

To opponents of banking, of course, this seemed like making burglary legal and then applauding the skill of the best burglar. Along with many others, Jackson felt that those doing the work of production should be the ones getting rich, not the lenders and speculators.

Jackson was elected to a first term as President as the people's champion against a decadent and corrupt elite. During the run-up to his second term "the Bank was the leading issue" (1947: 11). 'The Bank' was the Bank of the United States, a federally chartered Bank which had come to act as a Central Bank, restraining State-chartered banks from creating

---

[115] "It was evident to the anti-bank people that banking was a means by which a relatively small number of persons enjoyed the privilege of creating money to be lent, for the money obtained by borrowers at banks was in the form of the banks' own notes. The fruits of the abuse were obvious: notes were overissued, their redemption was evaded, they lost their value, and the innocent husbandman and mechanic who were paid in them were cheated and pauperized." (Hammond, 1947: 5)

too much credit. And here a mighty conflict of interest arose. Jackson, it seems, was even more pro-state than he was anti-bank. His obsession was to destroy the Federal Bank; but by destroying the Federal Bank without changing the system, he unleashed money-creation by state-chartered banks on a grand scale.[116]

Jackson was something of an innocent in politics. He was supported and surrounded by a bunch of able political manipulators keen to destroy the Federal Bank for entirely different reasons: they wanted to get their hands on as much created credit as possible (from local, State-chartered banks) and the Federal Bank was holding them back.

It seems his powerful supporters ran rings round Jackson. His destruction of the Federal Bank allowed credit-creation full rein. In Bray Hammond's words, he "fomented the very evils he deplored and made the Jacksonian inflation one of the worst in American history." Hammond's verdict: Jackson "professed to be the deliverer of his people from the oppressions of the mammoth, but instead he delivered the private banks from federal control and his people to speculation. No more striking example could be found of a leader fostering the very evil he was angrily wishing out of the way. But this was the inevitable result of the agrarian effort to ride two horses bound in opposite directions: one being monetary policy and the other states' rights" (1947: 9).

The victory of banking was, in Bray Hammond's eyes, inevitable. "In an austere land or among a contemplative and self-denying people they [anti-banking principles] might have survived but not in one so amply endowed as the United States and so much dominated by an energetic and acquisitive European stock." Banking made "capital accessible in abundance to millions of go-getting Americans who otherwise could not have exploited their natural resources with such whirlwind energy" (Ibid.)

In this way, power was increasingly in the hands of professional profit-takers "whose interest" – to quote Adam Smith (1776) again – "is never exactly the same with that of the public, who have generally an interest to deceive and even to oppress the public, and who accordingly have, upon many occasions, both deceived and oppressed it."

Anti-banking writers who are still heard-of today tend to be famous for things other than their opposition to banks. After John Taylor (1753-1824), there was Daniel Raymond (1786-1849). He is often referred to

---

[116] Not until 1913 was a central bank re-established: the Federal Reserve.

with pride as 'America's first important political economist' but strangely his opinions are not often quoted and there is no modern edition of his major work, *Elements of Political Economy* (1823). Raymond was hostile to the collusion between banks and governments and most of his insights are forgotten. In fact, he was unequivocally critical of banks. They are, he wrote:

> artificial engines of power, contrived by the rich for the purpose of increasing their already too great ascendency, and calculated to destroy that natural equality among men, which no government ought to lend its power to destroying. The tendency of such institutions is to cause a more unequal division of property, and a greater inequality among men, than would otherwise take place; which necessarily bring in their train, as has already been shown, poverty, pauperism and misery on some portion of the community. (1823: 121)

In Raymond's day, banks had to supply gold in exchange for notes when asked. He points out that if the public did not occasionally ask for gold, banks could manufacture unlimited amounts of credit-money: in which case "they would long before now have become possessed of every foot of property in the country, which would have been paid to them in the shape of interest for their money." (p.179)

And of course, excessive production of new money, for profit-taking rather than circulation, leads to inflation, making everyone poorer except those who are actively making money with the new money. This is how Raymond puts it:

> The ordinary race of politicians supposes, that a scarcity of money arises from a deficiency in quantity, but this is a manifest error. Money is always plenty or scarce in proportion to the rapidity with which it circulates, and not in proportion to the quantity in the country. A million of dollars which should change hands in the regular course of business once a day the year round, would have a much greater effect in making money plenty, than ten millions would, which should change hands, only once in ten days; or even a hundred millions which should change hands only three times a year. When there is a rapid consumption, and of course a brisk demand for all the products of labour, and for labour itself, there will be a rapid circulation of money, and it will be plenty. The object of governments should therefore be, to promote the circulation and not to

increase the nominal quantity of money. If the quantity of money is augmented by the actual increase of the quantity of value, it will be beneficial; because, this can be effected only by stimulating the industry of the people. But to increase the nominal quantity of money without increasing the actual quantity of value, is prejudicial to the public, because it produces variation in the price of all commodities, and violates all existing contracts. Such fluctuations in the price of property always ruin a vast many people, and cause a vast deal of suffering. (pp.240-241)

Many of Raymond's insights and observations (such as his debunking of Adam Smith on banking) deserve enshrinement in some imaginary Economics Hall of Fame. Instead, they have been consigned, along with much other wisdom, to dusty old books in reserve collections.

The next theorist still talked of is William M. Gouge (1796-1863), revered today as a historian of banking but forgotten for the work he really cared about: his critique of the banking system and his proposals for its reform. He published many articles on this and founded a periodical to further his ideas, *The Journal of Banking*. He, too, saw the promise of America dissolving into a plutocracy fuelled by banks. He argued that if banking was reformed, the political promise of America could return once again to be fulfilled. Here is how he ends his most significant book:

We have heretofore been too disregardful of the fact that social order is quite as dependent on the laws which regulate the distribution of wealth, as on political organization. Let us remove these excrescences by which our excellent form of Government is prevented from answering its intended end, and our country will become, 'THE PRAISE OF ALL THE EARTH'. (1833)

Gouge recognised that money created by banks is what we would now call 'fake debt': "The natural order of things is reversed and interest is paid to the Banks on evidences of debt due by them." Gouge pinpointed the part played by bank-money in the development of corporations. It gives "to corporations a power which enables them to exercise an influence on society nearly as great as that which was exercised by feudal lords in the Middle Ages." As an expert on banking and banking history, Gouge had interesting suggestions for reform (as did other early

Americans) some of which are remarkably similar to those put forward by reformists today.[117]

Friedrich List

In the meantime, an economist had arrived from Germany who would inspire the entrepreneurial community to an orgy of excitement and self-admiration. As fate would have it, he was the same economist who would later father nationalist and racialist economics in Germany: Friedrich List (1789-1846). Reading List after reading Taylor, Raymond or Gouge is to jump from the warm and heady waters of imagined justice into an acid bath of *realpolitik*.

Friedrich List was born in Wurttemberg, Germany. As a young man, he was first imprisoned and then exiled from Wurttemberg for promoting constitutional reform. He arrived in the United States in the company of General Lafayette, a hero of both the American and French Revolutions. In Lafayette's company, List met many influential people, and in 1827 he published two pamphlets: *Outlines of American Political Economy* and *A Speech given at the Philadelphia Manufacturers' Dinner*.

List's biographer Henderson writes: "With the publication of his two pamphlets, List found that he had suddenly become a public figure... List was now recognised in the United States as an authority on fiscal policy and a leading champion of the policy of protection," (1983: 154). List's American promoter wrote that his letters were "favorably received by the most eminent men of the country, such as James Madison, Henry Clay, Edward Livingston, etc."[118]

Competition between nations, List wrote, means that a nation must seek international power. List claimed that his version of 'American political economy' was descended in part from the vision of founding father Alexander Hamilton. American industrialists and bankers greeted him with rapture; not because his work was a revelation, but because it was applause for what they were doing anyway.

---

[117] In his later writings, Gouge (1843a and b) tried to accommodate banking to Adam Smith's doctrine of 'real bills' so that bank notes would represent already-existing value. If this were the case, he argued, 'we should enjoy all the real advantages of the present system, and be delivered from all of its evils.'

[118] George A. Matile from the Preface to (List, 1856).

A nation, List explains, is a "separate society of individuals who... constitute one body, free and independent, following only the dictates of its own interest as regards other independent bodies, and possessing power to regulate the interests of the individuals constituting that body" (1827: 9-10). Who, in List's scheme of things, would exercise the "power to regulate the interests of individuals"? The answer would seem to be "a National Convention, composed of men of all parties, for the sole purpose of elevating the welfare of the country" which in context sounds very like a committee of plutocrats, assisted by compliant politicians and economists (p.7). Recognising the inevitability (and under certain circumstances desirability) of war, the nation must pursue power and self-sufficiency as well as prosperity. (1904: 148)

In a series of outrageously sycophantic passages List seduced his American audience of manufacturers and plutocrats with the promise that the United States – "where heroes are sages and sages rulers" (1827: 3) – would eventually dominate the world and, afterwards, impose a global order of peace and plenty.

> ...in after ages this country will proclaim true cosmopolitical principles. When it shall count a hundred millions of inhabitants in a hundred states; when our industry will have attained the greatest perfection, and all the seas will be covered with our ships; when New York will be the greatest commercial emporium and Philadelphia the greatest manufacturing city in the world; when Albion [*England*] in industry and wealth will be nearly equal to Pennsylvania, and no earthly power can longer resist the American Stars; then our children's children will proclaim freedom of trade throughout the world, by land and sea. (p.5)

Monopoly and created credit would both be helpful for this task. List recognises that bank-credit is created money: in his American pamphlet *Outlines* he accepts that banks issue at least three times the amount in credit as they carry in cash. He then, in a widely touted illusion of the time, declares that this credit is based in property and land:

> If only a third part of these circulating notes represent cash, what do the other two parts represent? For, being nothing more by themselves than stamped rags, nobody would take them if they would not represent anything of value. They represent a nominated quantity of money consisting in the value of property and land. (1909: Appendix, 8)

The illusion that claims against banks were somehow, mystically or magically, backed by property and land was repeatedly shown up during the early nineteenth century, which was a great age of bank crashes, each crash leaving behind it a trail of dispossessed depositors and note-holders.[119] 'Land-banks' were tried but they always failed, because at the key moment the land was never available to back them up. It seems List was indulging in a convenient fantasy, as so many of us do when we are advocating something evidently discordant with observed reality.

In reality, money that is mere numbers or paper relies on law and active government to keep it valuable; on good and active government to make it an instrument of justice; and on bad and active government to turn it into today's 'tyranny of fraud'.

World domination by America, as foretold by List, was bound up with fantasies of racial superiority. Generally, List likes to imply that people can be "led, by a desire of enjoyment, to laborious habits and to improvements of their intellectual and social conditions" – but only, it would seem, white people (1827: 25). For America, he recommended the "exportation of black people" which "though diminishing our numbers, may be considered as beneficial; it is an exportation of weakness and not of power" (p.24). A page later, List characterises Mexicans as indolent. Taken as a whole, List's work is like a racist glove waiting for an iron fist to be put inside. What America held back from doing in this regard, Germany went on to fulfil.

Twenty years later List was back in Germany, advocating German dominance in Europe, beginning with the absorption of Denmark and Holland: "These two nations belong, besides, by their origin and by their whole history, to the German nationality" (List, 1856: 265).

In 1841 List wrote his magnum opus, *The National System of Political Economy*. Six years later, after a series of business and political failures, he killed himself.

In nationalist economics, freedom belongs to the powerful and justice is a lost and wandering soul. It was left to outsiders like Henry Carey

---

[119] Perhaps List was implying that in a world without limited liability, land and property of owners of banks could be sold to pay off creditors (if there was enough of it); but in practice, limited liability was already pretty effectively enshrined in contract, and owners and directors of banks enjoyed many other types of protection against the claims of depositors. Ruined depositors were, repeatedly, the actual consequence of bank failure.

Baird, a publisher of scientific and technical books, to meditate on the injustice of 'fictitious' or 'imaginary' credit as an engine of international power.[120] In 1876, Baird wrote and self-published *Inflated Bank Credit as a Substitute for Current Money of the Realm*, a pamphlet explaining how created credit enabled and supported the immense power of Britain's commercial and military empire. What the Romans had done with the sword, he wrote, was achieved in the British Empire with created credit: a means of locating ownership with a conquering few.

Amasa Walker

Our fourth major economist, Amasa Walker (1799-1875), was very outspoken about the effects of bank-money on society. He wished to re-instate political economy as a moral science, not as a technique for structuring society towards maximum production.

> That Political Economy is a science having nothing to do with morals or religion, nor in any way appertaining to human welfare, except so far as relates to the production and accumulation of wealth, is a common opinion... (but) I have felt desirous, throughout the following work, to show how perfectly the laws of wealth accord with all those moral and social laws which appertain to the higher nature and aspirations of man.

Amasa Walker's *The Science of Wealth* (1866) was published a hundred years after Adam Smith's *The Wealth of Nations*. Walker saw the United States dominated by an integrated system of banking, taxes and national debt, designed to take wealth from productive workers and relocate it with an equally integrated power of government, corporations and plutocrats. Building on the last chapter of Adam Smith's *Wealth of Nations*, Walker points out that National Debt is a great gift to the wealthy: they lose nothing by lending because they get government bonds in return. Meanwhile the interest on the debt – on money that the government spends – is paid out of taxes. As Montesquieu, Hume and Adam Smith and many others maintained (see Chapter Two), government debt "takes the wealth of the state from those who work, and gives it to those who are idle" (1866: 365-6).

---

[120] Among them are books by the man he was (presumably) named after, the economist Henry Carey.

His analysis of various types of currency is perhaps the most fascinating part of the book. The subject is vital to understanding how money-creation may either be impartial, or fuel inequality. Walker was writing at a time when at least *one* component of the money-supply was hard to manipulate and impossible to create: gold. His analysis of the types of currency then in use contains vital insights into how money may be manipulated by those in power.[121] As far as I know, there is no substitute for reading these chapters (and trying to understand them in a modern context) if one wants to understand the essential *simplicity* of money, and how the complexity of the system hides how it has changed money from a form of neutral property into a weapon-system for use in the interminable war of rich against poor.[122]

The huge effects on human life, society and activity of creating money-as-credit have been subsequently almost completely ignored in mainstream economics. Knut Wicksell, many years later, caused a stir in economics circles by noticing that there were two kinds of economy, a 'credit economy' and a 'cash economy'; but as far as I know he never followed up his observation with a thorough analysis.[123] Keynes made the same observation in his *Treatise on Money* (1930: Vol 2, 70) but he, too, pursued the matter no further.[124]

Amasa Walker saw the United States going down the same route that Britain had taken – towards impoverished masses and a hugely rich ruling class. In contra-distinction to today's plutocrats, who regard tax as theft from themselves, Walker sees government debt and banking as forms of 'taxation' that steal from the independent working poor and give to the

---

[121] An example would be the surreptitious and gradual replacement of gold by government-produced 'cash' as the 'reserve' in fractional reserve banking.

[122] A variation on this theme was noticed by Galbraith: "The study of money, above all other fields in economics, is the one in which complexity is used to disguise truth or to evade truth, not to reveal it." (1989: 15)

[123] I do not read Swedish or German, and not much of Wicksell's work has been translated into English.

[124] Keynes did, however, in a later essay, rather cryptically envisage a better future, when "All kinds of social customs and economic practices, affecting the distribution of wealth and of economic rewards and penalties, which we now maintain at all costs, however distasteful and unjust they may be in themselves, because they are tremendously useful in promoting the accumulation of capital, we shall then be free, at last, to discard." (Keynes, 1932).

rich, reverse-Robin-Hood style. He saw England as the most evident example of what happens after many years of government debt:

> What has become of that yeomanry, once the pride of the country? Their little estates have disappeared, have been swallowed up by the terrible system of taxation to which they have been subjected. The pleasant hedges which still surround the small enclosures, once constituting the freeholds of her yeomanry, may yet be seen in all parts of the country. They are the monuments of an industrious, brave, and independent class of men, now extinct. These lands are indeed tilled by the hands of their descendants, no longer yeomanry, but peasants, almost the paupers of the nation. (1866: 369)

By the end of the 19th century it was left to outsiders, like the industrialist William Berkey, to notice things which had once been common knowledge. "If the money-power is able to accomplish its designs in free, republican America, where else can the people hope to escape its bondage?" (2006: 361-2). In other words: if America adopts banking, what hope is there for the rest of the world? His premonition was perhaps even more spot-on than he realised. Soon, America would outdo Britain in rapacity across the world, and finance would be its principal weapon of war (Hudson, 2015a). Socialism would provide no respite, no protection: it adopted created credit as the main weapon in its arsenal of state control, as did communism and fascism.

Also, by the end of the century, hostile observations on money created by banking had been consigned to more or less total obscurity, even those that had been made by national heroes like Jefferson and Adams. What had happened?

The economics of nationalism had taken over and the notion of 'justice' in economics was in cold-storage. Nationalist economics is often called 'Romantic' – as if that makes it less bad. In reality, nationalist economics means a strong state, in collusion with industry and banking, using created-credit first to subordinate workers at home and dominate peoples, territory and resources abroad.

Created-credit is the ideal imperialist instrument. With money created out of nothing, it purchases labour and natural resources from countries less sophisticated in the art of 'robber banking' and exploits them for the benefit of a few in the home country.

Arguments for justice did, however, surface again in the 20th century during the Great Depression. Economists such as Irving Fisher and Henry C. Simons argued for reform of the system; they gained attention from both public and politicians, but no real reforms took place. Efforts were made to relocate money at the poor end of society and these had some effect; but the system stayed as it was. Eventually, the Second World War arrived. With huge amounts of public expenditure going to soldiers, armaments workers and others involved in the war effort, desperate poverty and unemployment was temporarily relieved. After the war, America's influence and ownership of foreign assets increased enormously, its trading empire was enhanced, and prosperity returned somewhat. 'Trickle-down' became the duplicitous buzz-word for how money would reach the poorer elements of society. Meanwhile, the system ground on in its old familiar way, creating huge fortunes for some while depriving working people of just returns on their labour.

Henry C. Simons, most insightful and thoughtful of the reformers, committed suicide when the movement towards a restoration of justice in economic thinking was mostly abandoned by his fellow professional economists (Van Horn, 2014).

Again, simple pleas for justice and humanity had been defeated. Today, ignorance about money, its creation and the possibilities for reform have never been greater. The negative effects of money-creation by banks have also never been greater. Taylor's observations on banking are now long-forgotten, along with Adams's and Jefferson's ruminations on the descent of the U.S. from a republic into a 'tyranny of fraud'.

Fast-forward to today: vast corporations, having bought out means of production with bank-created money, have in large part moved production abroad. Stockholders profit more, while working people are deprived of work and livelihood.

Once the independent poor have been robbed into penury they must depend upon a 'welfare state' to stay alive. This gives the super-rich plenty of reason to complain when some of their money is diverted to supply those they have robbed with the 'bare necessities' of life; but in reality, they are assisted in tax-avoidance and tax-evasion by highly-paid accountants, and the existence of tax havens: the burden of keeping alive those they have robbed falls mostly elsewhere, on tax-paying working and middle classes.

Since the eclipse of the early American economists, considerations of justice in economics have surfaced only sporadically. For many years now, mainstream economists have been denying or ignoring the fact that banks create money at all. This is an extraordinary stance: the fact has been established again and again at least since 1584, when Venetian senator and banker Tommaso Contarini explained it to Venetian politicians. Resistance by economists to this first-base truth makes it easy for them to avoid even discussing the destructive outcomes of creating money this way. Recently, economist Richard Werner (b. 1967) has been waging almost a one-man war against this tendency, meticulously proving that banks do in fact create money via statistical, mathematical and legal analysis (2014 and 2016).

The destructive outcomes of allowing banks to create, rent out and destroy money are the subject of the next chapter.

CHAPTER SEVEN

Secrets, Ignorance and Lies: Money, Credit and Debt

It is well enough that people of the nation do not understand our banking and monetary system, for if they did, I believe there would be a revolution before tomorrow morning.

Attributed to, amongst others, Henry Ford.

The tyranny of fraud is not less oppressive than that of force.

John Taylor of Caroline, Virginia (1814).

Our money system relies on people not understanding it. If people understood it, they would demand reform.

The most outrageous falsehoods are propagated daily about money and banking. Here are one or two examples: the first is the middleman narrative: "A commercial bank is fundamentally nothing more than a middleman to put these two groups of people (*investors and entrepreneurs*) together in an efficient way" (Cohan, 2017: 27).

This untruth is repeated regularly in education and the media, and most people believe it. However, the 'middleman' story is refuted repeatedly and explicitly by authorities who know about the system and are honest.

Here are four authoritative refutations of the 'middleman' narrative:

1) The Bank of England (2014: 2):

> One common misconception is that banks act simply as intermediaries, lending out the deposits that savers place with them...[this] ignores the fact that, in reality in the modern economy, commercial banks are the creators of deposit money. ...Rather than banks lending out deposits that are placed with them, the act of lending creates deposits - the reverse of the sequence typically described in textbooks.

2) Not all deposits are created by bank lending, of course; once money has been created, it circulates, is deposited and withdrawn just as we expect it to be. But when money is created, numbers are simply written into deposit accounts. Abbott Payson Usher, banking historian (1943):

> The essential function of a banking system is the creation of credit, whether in the form of the current accounts of depositors, or in the form of notes. The form of credit is less important than the fact of credit creation.

The 'essential' point here is that if banks weren't able to create digits for lending, their business would be less profitable to themselves, to governments and to 'capitalists'.

3) Joseph Schumpeter, economist (1954: 1114):

> It is much more realistic to say that the banks 'create credit', that is, that they create deposits in their act of lending, than to say they lend the deposits that have been entrusted to them.

4) Charles Franklin Dunbar, banking historian (1893: 48):

> deposits are created by the act of the bank when loans are increased and cancelled when loans are repaid.

The truth today is, banks do *not* lend money that already exists; they are not intermediaries or middlemen; they create deposit numbers (money) in the act of lending. This money then circulates, making payments and going in and out of people's deposit accounts.

Among the many bizarre results of this system is: if no one was borrowing from banks, there would be no money. (The interlinked nature of bank-money and debt was explored in Chapter Three.)

A second assertion which defies common sense and truth about banking is that it is responsible for affluence in the modern world. According to this version, banks fund science, technology, development, entrepreneurship, etc. and without them we would go back to the Middle Ages. Here is an example:

> Abandoning fractional reserve banking would be the ultimate throwing-out of the baby with the bathwater. It would be like, after a particularly bad motorway pile-up, legislating to outlaw motor vehicles and return to the horse and cart. (*The Times*, 10 June, 2018)

The fact is, banks create and lend mostly to speculators and predators; they do not often create and lend money to people starting businesses.[125] Those who initiate businesses tend to borrow privately and expand on the basis of profits. Only later do the 'big boys' move in with newly-created money. Banks do not create affluence, they plunder affluence and create the extreme inequality that plagues our world. Bank-created money also fuels a massive debt-creation industry ('financial services') devoted to creating value for rich people and poverty for others.

The intention behind this chapter is to draw lines of connection between the money system and some of the bad things that go on in our world. Some of these bad things are inherently bad, like war; others (such as inequality) are inevitable and acceptable in small doses, but bad in large ones.[126] An economist has made an analogy for the second type: a domestic cat is generally a well-loved addition to a home: enlarge it into a tiger, and it's not such a blessing.

The lines of connection I draw here are not simple lines of cause-and-effect. Many of the bad things listed happen anyway; the money-system just makes them worse. Most of my observations have been frequently made by others in the past. "It is a melancholy fact that each generation must relearn the facts of money in the bitter school of experience" wrote the French economist Maurice Allais (Feiwel, 1987: 491).

The paragraphs that follow address some of the malign effects of the way we create money. Each deserves at least a book, so this is just a summary.

Inequality

There is an abundant choice of statistics to express the huge inequality in our world today. One of the most telling is Oxfam's 2019 statistic that the 26 richest people on earth own more than the poorest half of the world's population, some 3.8 billion people.[127]

Essentially, banks create money for borrowers. How does this relate to inequality? Borrowers borrow either for consumption, or to make a profit.

---

[125] Many studies confirm this assertion: see, for instance, NEF's 'Our Friends in the City' available at: www.bit.ly/TPbr31

[126] Henry C. Simons puts it well: "A substantial measure of inequality may be unavoidable or essential for motivation; but it should be recognized as evil and tolerated only so far as the dictates of expediency are clear" (1948: 52).

[127] Reported in *The Guardian*: www.bit.ly/TPbr32

Loans for purposes of consumption are notoriously dangerous. Borrowers hope to be able to repay without having to sell their assets, but their hope is often misplaced.[128] As a result, many people who can't make ends meet get into debt and eventually lose assets. It is very easy to borrow if you have sufficient assets, because if you cannot pay back, the law will seize your assets and give them to the latest owner of your debt. Many individuals and corporations make it their business to buy debt on the cheap and extract as much as possible from the debtor with the help of the 'justice' system.

When money is borrowed for profit, on the other hand, both parties – bank and borrower – expect a profit, and have calculated they will get one. The bank expects interest on the loan: the borrower's profits must be extracted elsewhere, and more than cover interest payments. When the profit comes from productive industry it is either extracted from workers or added to production costs; either way, workers become less able to make ends meet. When the loan is made for speculation – say in housing – the price of property is driven up. Those who own property get richer.

As mentioned earlier, analyses of bank-lending indicate that very little new money is allocated to entrepreneurs, start-ups or people *initiating* productive businesses. According to economist John Kay, in the UK only 3% of new bank-money goes to productive businesses.[129]

A great deal goes to speculation in housing. This is what lies behind the 'housing boom', making it impossible for most young people today to own their own living accommodation. Meanwhile, created money makes people with assets richer, raising prices through speculative investment. A classic bubble – only this one, because of international and national support via money-creation by governments and banks, bursts repeatedly only to resume growing once again. Over the last forty-five years, property has risen in value many times faster than consumables like food, fridges and cars.

A great deal is also supplied to the finance industries, initiating and supporting forms of artificially created value for speculators and predators. After analysing the workings of finance, economic analyst

---

[128] The cycle of borrowing-and-loss is exacerbated by the tendency of bank-money to cause booms and busts: see below.

[129] "Lending to firms and individuals engaged in engaged in the production of goods and services – which most people would imagine is the principle business of a bank – amounts to about 3 per cent of that total" (Kay, 2015: 1).

Graham Hodgson (2013) concludes: "behind the operations of the finance sector, supposedly matching peoples' savings to the financing needs of businesses, stand the banks, hosing in cascades of money, from which all involved can siphon off remuneration." This money is, of course, newly created from nowhere.

A large amount of finance goes to the purchase of existing businesses. For these purchases to turn a profit, the business must be made more 'efficient': more productive, less expensive to run. Costs must be cut: wages reduced, suppliers put under pressure, working conditions economised on, humans replaced where possible by machines, computers, artificial intelligence, etc. Done in the name of increasing efficiency, the motive behind most of this activity is to increase profits for owners and reduce the amount going to those who already have less.

After new money has done its work, the original loan is repaid and the same amount of money disappears. More can then be created for another venture without affecting the ratio of credit to reserve.

It is difficult to quantify the effects of all this on inequality. A huge variety of activities are initiated by new money, each representing a different contribution to inequality. But it is perhaps worth noting that always and everywhere, the creation of new purchasing power out of nothing is an act of expropriation, no matter how dressed up it may be in the 'plausible ethics of productivity' or the seductive language of benevolent social management. New money is used to buy up, and profit from, the assets and labour of others. New money also causes inflation, making genuine savings less valuable: in money terms, only those using the newly-created money are becoming more wealthy.

Extreme Inequality Seizes up the Economy

Imagine a café with a hundred customers: between them, they have a thousand dollars to spend. All are thirsty, but only one has bought a cup of coffee. The café owner is puzzled; he's not making any money. What he doesn't know is that one person has all the money and the others are all broke. Soon, the café owner will be broke too. That is a simple picture of economic paralysis due to inequality.

In extreme inequality, very little money circulates among the poor; most of it stays with the rich. In economic terms, this relates to Daniel Raymond's remark quoted earlier: "Money is always plenty or scarce in proportion to the rapidity with which it circulates, and not in proportion to the quantity in the country". Alexander Gray, an economic historian makes the point simply: "Production cannot go on unless there is a market for the goods" (1931: 326).

Extreme inequality is good for no one. At one end of the scale there is poverty, disempowerment and displacement. At the other end there are the corruptions of wealth and power. The most significant inequality is not in income but in assets: in 'what you are worth'. When the politician Bernie Sanders (candidate for the Democratic presidential nomination in 2016) said that "one family owns more wealth than the bottom forty percent of the American people" he was not talking about their income but about their accumulated wealth.[130] Income inequality, however, is more present in most people's minds and in their daily concerns. The effects of bank-created money on income inequality have been investigated by Graham Hodgson in a paper available online.[131]

Socialist redistribution puts some restraint on the growth of inequality, but there is a price: ever-growing dependence of citizens on government. The drift to inequality is better restrained by introducing some justice into the money system itself.[132]

The Effect of Inequality on Freedom

True freedom is crushed by great inequality. The majority become heavily dependent upon the few. In the words of the Victorian historian Lord Acton "Power tends to expand indefinitely … it is by the combined efforts of the weak, made under compulsion, to resist the reign of force and constant wrong, that liberty has been preserved." (1906: 51)

It is foolish to expect reform to come from above, from those in power. Yet again, this quote from Adam Smith (godfather of economics): "All for ourselves and nothing for other people, seems, in every age of the world,

---

[130] Sanders also pointed out that Walmart employees are paid so little that the government has to supplement their wages; thus the richest family in America is also the biggest profiteer from welfare payments.

[131] For a detailed analysis of how banking and finance contribute to income inequality see (/, 2013).

[132] "There is no doubt about the general character of the institution of property most friendly to freedom: it will be one which allows the widest distribution, and which discourages most effectively great and dangerous concentrations of power." (Oakeshott, 1991: 393)

to have been the vile maxim of the masters of mankind" (1776: Bk 3, Ch IV). Or Michael Oakeshott: "It is mere foolishness to complain when absolute power is abused. It exists in order to be abused" (1991: 395).

Humanity under Threat: A Characteristic of Today's Inequality

Extreme inequality feeds and controls many of the evils that threaten our world. Our civilisation has come to resemble the Titanic: inequality is the fog; icebergs are all around. Nuclear weapons and global warming are two looming icebergs. While many civilisations have come to grief without threatening the continuity of human life on Earth, the power of humanity to self-destruct has grown enormously in recent years.

Our monetary system gives power to those individuals, undoubtedly a minority in any community, who are driven by an insatiable appetite for 'more' rather than by a desire to contribute and be rewarded with sufficiency. Their overweening influence and power shift the moral focus of the community towards selfishness and greed, and away from community and concern for the common good.

The globalisation of power has concentrated power in political-financial elites for whom 'getting more' seems to override all other considerations. Political representatives are supposed to represent us all, but in reality they represent the interests of the powerful factions that fund them. In the context of this book, the illusion that representative government is a form of democracy serves two functions: it deceives the people into thinking they are in control, and it allows elites (who also believe the illusion) to think that it is the people's stupidity, rather than their own duplicity, which has led us to the edge of self-destruction.

Already in 1814, John Taylor noted: "representation in England, designed to shield the people against oppression, has been gradually changed into a representation to shield oppression against the people" (1814: 607). Representatives are chosen by powerful factions, and a choice between them is offered up to voters: that is hardly 'democracy'.

Nature Degraded and Destroyed

Devastation of the environment by industrial methods of farming is apparent today across the globe.

The role of bank-money in this is clear. Land traditionally farmed is purchased with newly-created money and given over to industrial farming methods which replace humans with computers and machines, using chemical poisons and mass animal husbandry.[133] All of these practices contribute severe harm to the environment and to our future.

The devastations wrought by industrial farming are justified by the assertion that food is produced more cheaply this way. This assertion is, however, challenged in many recent studies.[134] Even if the assertion were true, the simple fact of 'cheaper food' leaves out certain elements which give the lie to its supposed 'economic utility'. For instance: those who work on industrial farms experience depression and illness; food produced by industrial farming is less nutritious than traditionally produced food, and increasingly carries diseases such as campylobacteriosis and salmonella.[135]

> Our current food system has a number of hidden costs to the natural environment and human health, far outweighing the benefits of cheap food. These costs aren't paid for at the grocery checkout counter, but eaters and consumers still bear the brunt of this financial burden through taxes and healthcare costs."[136]

Furthermore, industrialised agriculture increases our dependence on fossil fuels and contributes to the huge loss in diversity of species which, in the view of UNESCO, threatens our future as much as climate change.[137]

A simplified picture of the effects is a farm of, say, eight hundred acres: whereas once it sustained dozens of families, it may now be owned by one person and worked by one other. Traditional methods produce more and use more human labour, restoring some human connection with the world around us – not such a bad thing perhaps?

---

[133] It is wrong to think, "well, they could have borrowed the money anyway, banks or no banks". The earlier example of William III trying to borrow for war, shows that when money is dispersed in private hands, borrowing for destructive activities is much harder, and often impossible. When individual decisions are involved, as opposed to corporate profit-led criteria, morality is a significant factor.

[134] For instance, (Massy, 2018) and 'Regenerative Organic Agriculture and Climate Change', available at rodaleinstitute.org.

[135] 'Cheap Food Costs Dear' published online by cipf.org.

[136] www.bit.ly/TPbr33

[137] "Biodiversity is the living fabric of our planet. It underpins human wellbeing in the present and in the future, and its rapid decline threatens nature and people alike." (UNESCO, 2018)

As usual, the virtues of 'efficiency' and 'productivity' hide the true driving forces behind the changes, which have been, over the centuries, to increase profits for owners and investors.

Nor is the ocean exempt: industrialised fishing is robbing it, too, of diversity and life, and pollutants are filling it with plastics and poison.

Economic Expansion and the Environment

Economies based on bank-money require constant expansion and growth. Why?

The principal reason is that when banks create the money supply, inequality grows more acute. As money is taken out of circulation and stockpiled in ever greater quantities, the amount of money available for spending among working citizens decreases. Less and less money gets spent on consumption and production of all kinds: someone with a trillion dollars can only consume a little more than someone with a thousand dollars. In a bank-money economy, money for spending can only be put back among ordinary citizens by redistributive taxation (but rich people are good at evading taxes), by the expansion of industry, or by war (see below).

The need for endless industrial expansion, which is an outcome of our money system, and the creation and satisfaction of more and more needs, which is an outcome of the ethos nurtured by our money system, cause pollution, destruction of nature and depletion of natural resources, and create life-threatening conditions for all humanity.

Economic growth comes in many different varieties. Human labour and consumption do not necessarily have to destroy the environment. Most cultural pursuits, for instance are not destructive of the environment. It seems the main culprit in environmental destruction is the amoral nature of corporations, devoted to maximising profits and exploitation of Nature whatever the consequences.

It is obviously a challenge to introduce advances of civilisation such as clean running water and electricity across the world without further destruction of the environment, but that is a challenge worth taking on.

Corporations and Loss of Moral Freedom

A corporation is a business organisation authorised to act as a single entity, separate and distinct from its owners, who are not liable for its misbehaviours. It is obliged to act in a way that maximises profits for those owners. It has most of the legal rights that individual humans enjoy, but behaves without the moral restraints that condition most human behaviour. Corporations buy up the world, often from those who have cultivated it responsibly for generations, and exploit it ruthlessly, driven by their legal obligation to maximise profits for shareholders. Unlike humans, corporations live (potentially) for ever and publish their accounts for all to see. This makes them ideal vehicles for borrowing huge amounts of money conjured from nothing by banks and their financial intermediaries. This money is used to purchase businesses built by others.

Their lack of moral restraint has been recognised as a danger since at least the 14th century. "How can a corporation be expected to behave itself, when it has no body to imprison or kick, no soul to damn?"[138]

Darwin reminds us that moral constraints are as important as intelligence for the survival of our species. "I fully subscribe to the judgment of those writers who maintain that of all the differences between man *(i.e. the human species)* and the lower animals, the moral sense or conscience is by far the most important,' he writes. On the development of these moral qualities, he writes: 'As they are highly beneficial to the species, they have in all probability been acquired through natural selection." (1875: 97 and 610)

Commercial profit-seeking corporations are an obvious threat to our continued survival. They institutionalise the worst and most dangerous tendencies of human behaviour, regulating and influencing human activity away from caring and morality towards maximising profit-taking.

National Debts

Laws allowing debt to be bought and sold favour people with wealth. When debt can be bought and sold, lenders to governments get a tradeable debt – a 'bond' – in return for what they lend. As Adam Smith pointed out, these bonds may be more valuable than the money lent.[139]

---

[138] The earliest version I have come across of this is from Giovanni d'Andrea (d. 1348): *"universitas non est capax poenae capitalis, corporalis, spiritualis . . . cum corpus animatum non habeat ad hoc aptum."*

[139] "The security which it (the government) grants to the original creditor, is made transferable to any other creditor; and from the universal confidence in the justice of the state, generally sells in the market for more than was originally paid for it. The merchant or monied man makes money by lending money to government, and instead of diminishing, increases his trading capital." (1776: Bk 5, Ch 3).

They are referred to by many economists as 'near-money' because they too are a form of negotiable debt and can be easily exchanged for real money.

In other words, the government borrows from rich individuals and spends it, but gives those rich individuals just as valuable 'near-money' in return. For hundreds of years, this practice has been derided by intelligent thinkers concerned with justice. Why not simply create the money themselves and spend it, rather than create valuable debt for the rich and charge taxpayers interest on the debt? The answer usually given by those who defend the procedure is that governments invariably create too much, leading to runaway inflation. This irresponsibility is easily suppressed, however, by empowering an authority with the specific duty of keeping the money supply constant (see the last chapter of this book, on Reform).

Not surprisingly, when money can be borrowed in this way, national debts grow enormously. They also create a bond of mutual self-interest between government and the rich which undermines democracy. This has been a consistent theme of public debts throughout the centuries.[140]

'Bonds' contribute in other ways to the wealth of the acquisitive rich. The new wealth becomes collateral for more borrowing – for the creation of more money and for a consequent inflation of the money supply, which robs everyone else (whose money becomes less valuable).[141] It especially robs taxpayers, because the interest payments are paid out of taxes.

After the English Parliament made debt a tradeable commodity (1694-1704) the national debt of England exploded. In the half-century after the foundation of the Bank of England, national debt went from 6% to 137% of national income (Mitchell, 1988). By 1783, "Three quarters of the annual budget of the government were absorbed in (paying) dividends" (Jenks, 1927: 14). Roughly the same sequence has occurred in other countries.

To quote again the words of Montesquieu (1748: Bk 22, Ch 17), national debt "takes the wealth of the state from those who work and giving it to those who are idle". Strangely, many of those classified by Montesquieu as 'idle' now work very hard indeed. The competition for unmerited wealth has become fierce and intense – and the rewards ever larger! Banks, too, willingly lend new money for governments to spend – until a nation's debt becomes too great for taxpayers to reliably fund it.

---

[140] See for instance Pezzolo (2004) from whom I quote in the Introduction.

[141] There has been fierce debate over whether bonds should be recognised as money. Perhaps the simplest resolution is to note the connection: bonds are used as collateral for the creation of new money.

There is an often-repeated cliché that 'the national debt is a way of making our children and grandchildren pay for what we use today'. This is only partially correct: everything, from missiles to food, has to be paid for before it is used. National debts are more a form of robbery than of delayed payment. They garner pre-existing money for the government, but they increase the money supply through the processes outlined above, increase wealth for the class of those who lend, and create debts for citizens and their dependents. Many, many writers have decried the injustice of this way of raising money when it is perfectly possible for governments to create money without borrowing.

National debts in some countries – the USA for example – have reached such dizzying heights that interest payments, even at very low rates, represent a substantial day-to-day drain on incomes, through the increase in taxation to pay the interest.

Private Debt: Booms and Busts

Booms and busts prepare the ground for large increases in private debt and inequality.[142] This happens because in times of plenty, people borrow with confidence that they will be able to repay. When hard times hit, they are not able to meet interest payments. The debt grows larger, and lenders claim their property in lieu of payment.

Banks respond to a boom by lending with gusto to all and sundry, creating new money on collateral of homes, businesses and other assets. For a while, all seems rosy: when the worm turns, profits and incomes dry up, and banks call in loans. Borrowers sell assets to pay off their debts, or banks seize their assets as collateral. Mortgages and reclaimed homes are a painful and well-publicised example.[143]

When banks call in debts, they are destroying money: deposit numbers simply vanish when a debt is repaid. Economists have called this the 'perverse elasticity' of bank-created money – money is easy-to-get when you don't actually need it, and near-impossible to get when you need it most (Lester, 1939: 291).

---

[142] The process used to be much more widely discussed: see for instance (Gouge, 1833: 26). He describes how during business cycles "Multitudes become bankrupt, and a few successful speculators get possession of the earnings and savings of many of their frugal and industrious neighbors."

[143] www.bit.ly/TPbr34

Today, when the quantity of debt (personal, corporate and national) is so large that it cannot be funded at conventional rates of interest, governments drive down interest rates, making money even cheaper to borrow for those who already have it. Speculation replaces investment: new money is used to create 'bubbles' in markets such as housing and real estate. In a world of created debt, there are always opportunities for speculators.

Huge profits may be taken by professional speculators before, during and after the business cycle. A skilful speculator will change techniques depending on the stage in the cycle, just as a skilled general knows how, where and when to do battle.

Busts ought to rectify the situation somewhat by reducing capital values and debt, but today's lawmakers and regulators intervene in the interest of keeping the system going. Of course, no one wants their bank to go bust! – so this is applauded. The outcome is that the system prospers while others are impoverished.

Authorities intervene in various ways to prop up the system. As well as massively reducing interest rates, governments and central banks prop up asset-values with devices such as 'quantitative easing'.[144] These efforts merely prolong the recession or depression. Inequalities increase – the rich getting richer, the poor poorer.

Eventually, economies have tended to emerge from recessions and depressions. Wars, expanding markets, debt reduction and default, falling capital values and other developments may each or all play a part in reducing or moderating inequality. Then, because no fundamental reform has been introduced, the cycle must begin again.[145]

Arms Proliferation and War

When money can be created and lent in private, governments indulge in the purchase and manufacture of arms without permission from their citizens. Governments naturally compete to acquire arms: if your neighbour gets missiles, you want them too. Arms become more and more threatening in both quality and quantity. There is pressure to test

---

[144] 'Quantitative easing//': the government creates 'reserve' money to buy assets such as its own debt; this reserve goes to the banks, relieving their over-stretched lending. For more, see Chapter Three.

[145] 'Business cycles' do not seem to have existed without bank-money and negotiable debt.

new weapons in 'battlefield conditions' and once a government has weapons, it is obviously more likely to use them.

Arms-manufacturing is a hugely profitable business for many countries. The five permanent members of the UN Security Council (China, France, Russia, the United Kingdom and the United States) are tasked with maintaining global peace and security, but companies based in these nations manufacture 71% of the world's arms, and the same arms companies contribute heavily to political campaigns (Fuller, 2015: 159). Sometimes the same government will fund several opposing factions in foreign disputes and wars: the activities of the United States in Central America under President Reagan are well-documented in this respect.

As a result, whole nations are devastated by wars that reinvigorate the domestic economies of superpowers.

Banks feed a vicious circle in arms production by eagerly creating new money for buyers, sellers and manufacturers. Citizens, unaware even of how money is created, remain unaware of how their economies are skewed to arms purchase and/or production. If debt was non-negotiable, governments would have to borrow pre-existing money to finance arms purchases. In normal times, 'lend me some money to buy weapons' is not a very popular request, particularly if a lender has to do without the money lent. (At the moment, if you lend money to a government you get a valuable bond in return – see Chapter Two.)

There is another very important factor that encourages arms production and war when money is created and destroyed as debt. As outlined above, inequality is a persistent problem in such economies. When people can no longer afford to buy all that is being produced, economies begin to seize up. In these circumstances, arms production and war act as economic stimulants. The arms industry and the armed forces employ people who do not make products for purchase by other citizens: even in America, citizens do not buy missiles and bombs. The wages of these arms-workers and soldiers are spent on products made by other workers. This spending stimulates the economy: in economic terms, it somewhat rectifies the 'demand deficit'.[146]

---

[146] In the Cold War 'arms race', the USA enjoyed a rare stretch of financial growth and stability: 5-10% per year for several decades (www.bit.ly/TPbr35). Today, Russia resorts to massive armaments production to restore spending money to a plundered populace; and North Korea (where the credit-creation facility belongs not to private banks but to the state) builds nuclear weapons despite, or perhaps because of, the poverty of its people.

In her book *Freedom and Necessity*, economist Joan Robinson outlines how arms spending was manipulated to provide financial stability during the 'Cold War' (1947-1991).[147] She also points out the moral perversity of the situation: "Rationality requires that the prime aim of policy should be to make war obsolete and to find alternative ways of dealing with the problems that give rise to it; but it is precisely the economic success of the military-industrial complex that puts the greatest obstacle in the way of any such attempt." (197: 87)

Arms production and war would not be economic stimulants in a just economic system; they would be a drain. In the system we have today, manufacturing arms to be sold abroad is even 'better' than producing them for home use: shareholders get richer, wages are spent in the home country, death and destruction occur somewhere else.

The 'economic stimulus' of arms production and war is responsible for pervasive hypocrisy in international affairs, as politicians and diplomats become salespersons for armaments to sustain the economy. Another outcome is 'proxy wars' fought in unstable countries, supported by nations who manufacture arms. Wikipedia's list of proxy wars, incomplete and out-of-date though it is, makes for depressing reading.[148] How many of these wars would have taken place if supplying arms was an expense, rather than a source of profit and an economic stimulus, to the big powers?

Corruption

Corruption is made easy when money is created in private and out of nothing. In many countries, bankers and government officials are family relations, or involved in business together (See Dawisha 2015 and Burgis 2015). Some recent examples: In Bangladesh, "some $565 million in assets are said to have been looted from the state-owned BASIC Bank between

---

[147] "Whatever its causes, the consequence of the Cold War was to provide an outlet for government expenditure which did not compete with private enterprise and which did not saturate demand by producing anything that the public could consume." (Robinson, 1970: 86)

[148] A recent example: "In the first six years of the Obama administration the United States agreed to transfer nearly $50 billion in weaponry to Saudi Arabia" which then went to war with one of the poorest countries on Earth: Yemen. www.bit.ly/TPbr36

2009 and 2012, yet the scam's suspected mastermind, a former chairman of the bank, wasn't troubled by the anticorruption commission investigating the fraud, reportedly thanks to his political connections." Banks in Bangladesh "are regularly recapitalized by the government—to the tune of about $640 million for fiscal year 2014 and, it is expected, more than $700 million for fiscal year 2015" (Allchin, 2016). In Malaysia, a "billion-dollar political scandal" involves two brothers, a banker and the Prime Minister (Paddock, 2016). In Moldova, a large proportion of the wealth of the country has been looted and relocated with financial partners, mostly in Russia (Coffey, 2016).

Corruption of Capitalism

Capitalism supposedly depends upon savings lent to entrepreneurs. The idea is that banks provide a service to savers, by investing their savings. Today, however, genuine savings are dwarfed by bank-created money. Banks create money merely by typing digits. Savings kept in a bank do, it is true, mean that an equal amount of 'reserve' stays in the same bank; but this 'reserve' can form the backup for a much greater quantity of newly-created money.

As mentioned earlier in this chapter, new enterprise is mostly started by people who borrow elsewhere than from banks – perhaps from personal contacts, perhaps from crowd-sourcing via the internet. Banks do not like to take on excessive risk; they like to lend where the potential for profit-taking is obvious and the collateral solid. The comedian Bob Hope famously remarked, "A bank is a place that will lend you money if you can prove that you don't need it." As already stated, most bank-created money goes into speculation in asset prices, not to start-up business.[149]

Vast amounts of new money reduce not only the value of savings, but also the interest they can expect from being lent. All this makes a mockery of capitalism, its moral justification and practice.

Extremist politics

The monetary system allots huge and unaccountable powers to government. Party politics means that a change in government results in exploitation by a different cabal of interest groups – nothing more.

---

[149] http://neweconomics.org/2012/12/where-does-money-come-from/

It's an extraordinary fact that George Washington saw the development of party politics as early as 1796. He wrote his 'farewell address' as a letter to fellow-citizens warning of dangers ahead.

> The alternate domination of one faction over another, sharpened by the spirit of revenge, natural to party dissension, which in different ages and countries has perpetrated the most horrid enormities, is itself a frightful despotism. But this leads at length to a more formal and permanent despotism. The disorders and miseries, which result, gradually incline the minds of men to seek security and repose in the absolute power of an individual; and sooner or later the chief of some prevailing faction, more able or more fortunate than his competitors, turns this disposition to the purposes of his own elevation, on the ruins of Public Liberty.[150]

This has become true almost to the letter today. Citizens know they are being cheated but don't know how to put a stop to it, so instead of seeking reform they turn to unsavoury and dangerous monomaniacs, pathological power-seekers to lead them out of the mess. The world is becoming a more dangerous place, domestically and internationally. Examples of this today are everywhere.

Predation, National and International

As already mentioned, banks lend newly-created money to buy assets and labour; the borrower's projected profits must exceed the cost of borrowing. The moral virtue of 'efficiency' is invoked to justify loss of freedom and property among those who are bought out or dispossessed by the new money. This 'virtue' veils the historical motive, which has always been a simple one: for the borrower to get richer.

The collaboration between governments and banks is a simple one. Governments provide 'reserve' on demand for banks; banks create money and lend it to individuals, corporations, hedge funds and merchant banks for the profitable purchase of land, assets and labour.

Compound interest is a notorious device for robbing those unfamiliar with the tricks of finance. Money is created out of nothing, lent as debt, and high rates of interest are charged. When interest cannot be paid, it is added to the amount of the debt.

---

[150] www.bit.ly/TPbr48

Internationally, money lent is often a bribe to secure some trade advantage and gets squirreled away by corrupt officials, perhaps lodged back in the banking system of the country that lent it. Whole countries are impoverished by this practice. Nigerian President Obasanjo said at the G-8 summit, 2008: "If you would ask me 'what is the worst thing in the world?' I would say, 'compound interest.' We had borrowed around 5 billion dollars by 1985-6. To date, we have paid back 16 billion dollars. Now we are told we still have 28 billion dollars of debt."[151]

Colonisation, Past and Present

As seen in Chapter Four, bank-created money was a key ingredient in the practice of colonisation and the expansion of the British Empire. The creation of credit, the purchase of foreign assets and military power advanced together, until it could be said that 'the sun never set on the British Empire'. And the profits went to very few, just as they do today.

Economists tended in the past to be a little more honest about the process. For instance, a conversation reported by William Nassau Senior:

> foreigners can afford to give more for land than a native can... let a Turk once mortgage his land to a Christian protégé, and he will soon cease to have any property in it. In a very few years, the mortgage money will exceed the value of the fee simple. (1882: 195)

This has been going on for centuries: today it is the key ingredient in continuing colonial exploitation. A manifestation of this practice today is 'microcredit'. Small loans, advertised initially as a community benefit, are sold on to large finance companies who then claim the land for corporate agribusiness.[152]

Nor is colonisation dead: it continues by monetary means. Governments of countries with sophisticated banking industries are able to plunder internationally.[153] In the words of Henry C. Simons, "each

---

[151] Quoted in (Kennedy, 2012: 18). Also: "In 2008, developing countries were paying back $13 for every $1 they were receiving in development aid."

[152] See www.bit.ly/TPbr37 and, on the resulting suicides: www.bit.ly/TPbr38

[153] David Korten writes: "During my years working in Africa, Asia and Latin America, I came to realize that what we call 'development' is in fact a process of transferring control over the basic resources essential to daily life from the people who depend on them to foreign corporations, whose primary interest is financial gain." Foreword to (Kelly, 2012).

national currency is a fractional reserve bank" creating money for plunder (1948: 261). Because a nation's currency, while abroad, is effectively a claim on assets at home, the government hopes that the money will stay abroad or circulate as international currency and not return to purchase assets at home for foreign ownership. Unlike the debts that banks supposedly owe to their customers, debts to foreign countries do not disappear: they are not 'fake', because assets may be demanded in satisfaction. The U.S. currently owes China, Japan and other countries many trillions of dollars.

There are hidden disadvantages for poorer citizens in a nation whose currency becomes the international currency of choice. When a currency becomes overvalued, due to international demand for it as a store of value, manufactures of the home country become less competitive. Thus, American cars, fridges etc. enjoyed limited sales abroad for seventy years after the Second World War, compared to those manufactured (for example) in Japan or Germany.

~ ~

To sum up: The crimes committed by our system of money and finance are immense. Billions of people are dispossessed into poverty and debt; millions are on the move, their lands possessed and exploited by money created especially for that purpose; countless lives are being destroyed by wars, climate change and the degradation of our planet. Perhaps worst of all, our monetary system gives power to ambitious and irresponsible people driven by an insatiable appetite for 'more' rather than by a desire to contribute and to get 'enough' in return.

Negotiable debt has been a cause of crisis many times in the past. Debt slavery (Hudson, 2011) and tax farming (Beard, 2012) are other examples of debt made tradeable which had momentous consequences for civilisation. These will be looked at very briefly in the next chapter. We humans, it seems, learn little from past mistakes and therefore, as the expression goes, we are doomed to repeat them, each time more destructively.

Unless, that is, we wake up to the need for reform; which will be the subject of the final chapter.

CHAPTER EIGHT

Negotiable Debt: A Bit of History

This chapter is a quick summary and clarification of what happens when debt becomes negotiable. The focus is on money, but other aspects are referred to, highlighting the general undesirability of passing laws that allow debt to be bought and sold – that is, to allow debt to become 'negotiable'. There will be some repetition of material previously covered, for the sake of assembling it all in one place.

We all know what money is: a special, universal kind of property that passes from hand to hand to hand, whose purpose is to be exchanged for things that are up for sale. Because money can buy almost anything, hijacking the money supply is an obvious objective for any person or class wishing to become massively wealthy and/or powerful.

Thousands of years ago, when money was valuable metal, a simple way of doing this emerged. Having accumulated a quantity of the metal, a person or institution could issue 'promises-to pay' which were simply written notes promising to pay out valuable metal in exchange for the note (if requested to do so). These promises-to-pay might circulate as money – so long as the law supported them as valid claims on precious metal even while they passed from hand to hand to hand.

While the promises circulated, nothing needed to be paid out: the promises themselves acted as money. Because they were lighter and more compact, they were easier to use, and the gold and silver tended to stay put. And because the promises were valuable, they could be lent at interest. And because the precious metal was seldom claimed, lenders soon discovered that a great deal more could be promised than was kept in store.

The promises were, of course, a form of debt. Whoever issued them owed (in theory) the amount written on the note to anyone owning a 'promise-to-pay'.

Debt lent at interest! It's an idea that still seems strange and unfamiliar, even though it has dominated the world of wealth and power on and off for thousands of years. The words 'on and off' are important here, because we have records from times when debt was *not* a form of money, and evidence of how people lived in equality and security during those times.

This strange hybrid of debt and money is known today as 'credit'. We are all familiar with 'credit'; when we have money at the bank, we are 'in credit'. Legally, the bank owes us money. The bank's debt circulates as money, so it is best referred to as 'circulating credit'.

For credit to circulate and work as money, the state must support the idea that debt can be bought and sold. When debt can be bought and sold, it is called 'negotiable'. Negotiable debt and circulating credit are, therefore, the same thing; and credit can always be created by a powerful entity, merely by acknowledging a debt.

A state does not make debt 'negotiable' out of love for bankers and financiers: it does it because it increases the power and wealth of the state. Today, for instance, when debt is negotiable, a person who lends money to a government or a big corporation gets an asset in return – a 'bond' – which can be bought and sold. A lender loses nothing by lending, because the bond they get in return is as valuable as (or more valuable than) the money lent. When debt is 'negotiable' it makes it much easier for governments to borrow.

As explained in Chapter Two, there was a precise decade in modern history when records indicate that negotiable debt was explicitly established in law. This was in England, by the English Parliament, between the years of 1694 and 1704. At that time, Parliament consisted of rich males voted in by other rich males.[154] The most significant laws were the Bank of England Act (1694) and the Promissory Notes Act (1704). Licensing and regulations enable governments to limit the number of businesses allowed to join the money-creation game and to profit from it.

That was the first record of the practice being precisely authorised in historical documents, but the practice of negotiable debt has a much more

---

[154] "Each society in which commerce plays a role sooner or later has to face a strong demand to increase the circulation of credit." (Zimmermann, 1996: 59). 'The circulation of credit' is of course another way of saying 'negotiable debt'.

ancient history. This chapter aims to give a very brief survey of that history. Information on the subject is hard to come by, partly because time has obliterated much of the evidence. It has been very interesting nevertheless trawling through the literature on ancient economies, looking for signs of a history to the phenomenon.[155]

Ancient Forms of Circulating Credit

Starting with ancient Mesopotamia, we find temples and palaces holding all the gold and silver and renting out credit notes in the form of clay tablets that contain a negotiability clause: 'pay the bearer of this tablet' (Graeber, 2011: 214). This is covered in more detail in Chapter One. These tablets were a form of circulating credit.

In other words, the ruling order employed an ancient form of what we now call 'fractional reserve banking'. A much greater value in tablets was (presumably) issued than the palaces and temples held in precious metals. As already mentioned, in 1928 A.H. Pruessner wrote of these clay tablets that they introduced a new kind of money: records of indebtedness. "After this principle was once discovered, its advantages and benefits were found to be so manifold that nothing could stay its victorious advance."[156]

These 'advantages and benefits' were, of course, mostly to the ruling class. In ancient Mesopotamia, debt crises were a regular occurrence. Debtors who could not repay might be enslaved and sold by those who had lent them money. Rulers found it politic to cancel all debts every now and then. These 'debt jubilees' would add considerably to the popularity of the ruler. They were able to do this easily, because most of the debt was owed to themselves! Economist Michael Hudson points out that debt jubilees were in the rulers' interest for more reasons than just increasing their popularity. First, war was a regular occurrence: armies of slaves are not passionate fighters and are liable to turn on their masters. Second, debt jubilees prevented the growth of a class of 'creditor-entrepreneurs' whose power might grow to rival that of the rulers (Hudson, 2002: 37).

---

[155] Not many historians go into detail of whether debts were transferable, let alone analyse the effects. Economists steer clear of the subject: John Maynard Keynes (1930) and Milton Friedman (1948) both wrote about how banks create money early in their careers only to drop the subject later.

[156] The 1920s were the last days of substantial honesty in created debt. It is significant that Pruessner was not a recognised economist.

Moving on to Ancient Greece, historians used traditionally to assert that its economy and payment systems were based on coin. Then in 1992, Edward E. Cohen, himself a banker, pointed to the overwhelming evidence that by the 4th century in ancient Athens, banks and bank-credit were very significant indeed. His book *Athenian Economy and Society: A Banking Perspective* is dense and learned.[157]

It is significant that during the 4th century in Athens, inequality grew and social equality among free men diminished. So-called 'sycophants' would puff up and bring down wealthy citizens for profit, stirring up public envy and greed, and finding reasons why the courts should confiscate the wealth of rich citizens (Burckhardt, 1963: 304-5). In this new political and social climate, "the great Athens of old was gone and beyond recall". The Athenian city-state became weak and vulnerable to the growing power of Macedonia to the north, which eventually subjected Athens. Democracy as a form (rather than an element) of government was then submerged for at least a thousand years.

Moving on to Ancient Rome, recent books and scholarly articles have established that it, too, had fractional reserve banking.[158] But another form of negotiable debt in the Roman Empire has attracted more attention over the years, and that is tax farming. Tax farming occurs when a ruling order finds it tiresome to organise tax-collection: instead, it auctions off the tax-debts of citizens to private enterprise, to 'tax-farmers', referred to in Latin as *'publicani'*. It is a limited form of debt negotiability, but it had stupendous consequences.

With the help of state-violence, these tax-farmers collected the taxes plus a bit extra – or more often, a *lot* extra – for themselves. According to tax historian Charles Adams (1993), Roman tax-farmers formed the first private business corporations, and their shares were bought and sold in the Forum. The ruling class invested heavily in their companies, and individuals became fantastically rich.

Historian A.H.M. Jones (1968) comments that this selling-off of debt corrupted the political and financial system of the Roman republic from top to bottom. Provincial governors became greed-obsessed, top senators

---

[157] And in (Harris, 2008) Cohen writes "Athens avoided the artificial (dare we say 'primitive'?) condition of the United States … Athenian bankers and vendors generated 'money' without the legalistic dependence on physical metals familiar from the recent history of the United States." (pp. 82-3)

[158] See www.bit.ly/TPbr39, also (Collins & Walsh, 2014).

invested in profitable tax-extortion, and ordinary working people were driven into debt. Parallels with today's privatisations spring to mind.

Charles Adams blames these tax-farmers not just for the downfall of the Roman Republic; but also, and more momentously, for the eclipse of republican and democratic forms of government for fifteen hundred years.[159]

A Respite

In Europe, the so-called Dark Ages provided some respite from these extortions. Trade became difficult, and rulers could only consume what was locally produced. There wasn't much point over-exploiting peasants and craft workers if you couldn't sell their produce abroad (Pirenne 1948 and 1969).

By the time what we call 'civilisation' began to return with the Middle Ages, the Church was enforcing harsh laws against usury. Usury meant lending at interest – as covered in Chapter Four, they did little analysis of how banking actually *creates* money. But the Church had authority; it had become not just a moral influence, but also a worldly power.

Powerful princes and merchants found ways around the Church's laws of usury.[160] But monarchs and barons were wary of giving power to the growing merchant class and were as likely to rob as to borrow from them. Frequently they did both – by borrowing and then defaulting on their debts.

As trade returned, so the merchant class grew in strength, and pressure grew again for debt to be legally recognised as a negotiable commodity. After several centuries of pushing against the existing order, the merchant class was victorious and, today, all legal systems provide some way in which debt can be bought and sold.[161]

---

[159] (Adams, 1993: 90). "All representative government passed away. Caesars would rule for the next fifteen hundred years. And for this tragedy, who and what was to blame? The tax system of the *publicani*."

[160] See various works by Raymond de Roover, for instance, 'The Scholastics, Usury, and Foreign Exchange' in (de Roover, 1975).

[161] "The development of explicit and unrestricted negotiability covers a period of nearly two centuries" (Usher, 1943: 98). This book contains the classic account (pp. 1-107) of the slow change in Europe.

To finish off this micro-survey, there is one small tale left to relate, and that is of 18th-century France.

In 1720, the same year as the South Sea Bubble in England, a Scotsman named John Law brought financial disaster to France (this story is touched on in Chapter Five). He concocted a wild scheme involving bank-credit and national debt, consolidated into shares in a project to develop Mississippi. This resulted in the Mississippi Bubble, which bankrupted a lot of wealthy Frenchmen. After this, the French were wary of banks for a century or more.

Tax-farming, on the other hand, suited the French monarchy well. Extortion of the peasantry and the middle classes was conducted via tax-farming, and this helped bring on the Revolution in France. "To collect taxes, the government delegated its coercive police powers to the syndicate" (White, 2004: 647). This made tax farmers particularly unpopular and in May 1794, 28 former tax-farmers were guillotined.

After the Revolution, the government lacked a developed credit and banking system to finance its adventures, so it tried the clumsy mechanism of printing money – which led to grotesque inflation. On the back of this, Napoleon came to power. He took France to war, relying on plunder and taxation of conquered territories to finance his armies. His British enemies relied on created credit. An article (Bordo & White, 1991) in the *Journal of Economic History* describes how the war was won by British credit: once again, credit played a vital role in warfare.

Created credit in the form of negotiable debt has a double involvement with war. First, because money can be summoned in huge amounts out of nowhere, war can (in the early stages) be easily paid for. Second, as explained in Chapter Eight, when money is created by banks, preparation for war is a healthy stimulus to the economy rather than a drain. Economist Joan Robinson explains in *Freedom and Necessity* how huge expenditures on arms kept Western economies healthy during the Cold War. Taxation paid for arms and military activity, supplying money to workers who would spend it on the products of other industries, thereby stimulating the economy.

The complexities and evils of our present-day monetary system arise from a very simple foundation: the negotiability of debt. When debt is negotiable, powerful entities create very large amounts of value merely by acknowledging debt. This becomes very relevant when considering how the system might be reformed.

CHAPTER NINE

Reform

Anyone who has read this far probably feels that reform would be a good idea. On paper, it would be a simple matter: cancelling unjust laws that support negotiable debt. It is this reform that is vitally needed; all others are tinkering at the edges and will be easily evaded (as they have been in the past) by new devices to exploit negotiable debt.[162]

But reform will be more than very hard to achieve. Powerful interest groups will lose out: they depend on negotiable debt for their monopoly on wealth and their political control. To make things worse, victims who would benefit from reform mostly do not understand the role that negotiable debt plays in destroying the world and our future. As a result, those who are robbed by the system and its practitioners turn to the wrong people to put things right: to nationalists and totalitarians, who are not inclined to reform the system, but will use it to increase their own power and line their own pockets. So the picture painted here is gloomy, but towards the end of the chapter positive and hopeful signs will be considered.

Fundamental reform would mean, as well as cancelling unjust laws, reducing the vast fortunes accumulated with the help of those laws. There is precedent for this kind of reform: in Germany after the Second World War, the occupying forces and the West German government imposed reductions on the vast fortunes accumulated by Nazi financiers. The economy sprang back to life (more on this later in this chapter).

What chance is there of fundamental reform along these lines? Most reformers agree that the change most needed is a change to our moral and aspirational values.

---

[162] See examples in Chapter Six. New devices have now been invented by advanced mathematicians in league with financiers, so negotiable debt instruments now amount to a sum many times greater than total global production.

For thousands of years, ruling orders have found it acceptable, even heroic, to steal from vulnerable people. At home, this can be done via laws (for instance Enclosure Acts); internationally, it is done by war. But the world is changing. War is regarded as a blot on civilisation and no longer as a heroic endeavour. Ordinary people have (a little) more say in what goes on. There is more access to information. Advanced weapons systems have become a well-recognised threat to us all. And perhaps most importantly, women have been gaining in influence and power.

For many thousands of years, men were more-or-less completely in charge. It takes an act of wilful blindness to see no connection between this and the tenor of society – its moral character and the direction it takes. Over the last century and a half, anthropologists such as Johann Jakob Bachofen (1815-1887) and Marija Gimbutas (1921-1994) have suggested the following scenario: before our planet became overcrowded with humans, we were more peaceful among ourselves, and women were the dominant sex. When the planet became overcrowded, humans began to fight over resources and males took over because they are more inclined to fighting and violence.[163]

Mainstream anthropologists have tended to mock this narrative, but a recent report says it is once again gaining ground after DNA studies have supported it with new evidence.[164]

Today, conflict between two moral attitudes is becoming ever more stark and obvious. One says: "Grab what you can. Lie, cheat, steal, get rich. Care nothing for other people. Chase enjoyment." The other says "Respect justice and truth, do what is right, act out of love and care for the world and its peoples." Of course, the choice here is not simple and final; most people act on both these moral impulses at different times and in different circumstances.

In today's changing conditions, many people are coming to realise that acts of accommodation rather than violence are necessary if we are to survive and prosper as a species, and that we must look after the environment rather than ruthlessly exploiting it.

However, in a world structured around the old values of war and competing weapons systems, of predatory finance and industrial

---

[163] Bachofen's book is translated into English as *Mother Right*. Gimbutas wrote many books including *The Civilization of the Goddess*.

[164] 'The Tribe That Re-wrote History' in *New Scientist*, 30 March, 2019.

exploitation, women tend to succeed by outcompeting men at their own game. These patriarchal structures need to change. The money system is one of them – perhaps the most important.

Why Reform?

Financial reform will be hard to achieve, so it's worth trying to imagine how the world would benefit once money is created equitably.

It is hard to answer this by looking at the past. Historically, as soon as 'surplus value' is being created – in other words, as soon as workers are producing more than is necessary for their survival – powers have emerged to seize the surplus for themselves. So far, these powers have been 'the sword' and the 'money-power', often in competition. The money-power tends to take over as trade and commerce become more important. Exploitation by the money-power is subtler and less obvious than exploitation by the sword.

A fairer distribution of surplus value does, however sometimes occur historically in gaps between the dominance of these two powers. In 17th-century England, for instance, feudal powers were in decline and the money-power was not yet fully developed. For a brief time, property was more equally distributed and ordinary people were more prosperous. This temporary shift towards equality lasted into the next century, long enough for observers like Voltaire, Hume and Montesquieu to be astonished and impressed by it.[165] A century later, it was the opposite; foreigners were noticing the terrible poverty of the English working classes, both agricultural and industrial (see Chapter Two).

So what are the characteristics of a just money supply that circulates without favouring any party or power-base?

Power would cease to be the preserve of the rich and ruthless, and dwell among the people; not just political international power, but the power of everyday decision-making which affects people's lives. The ruling orders like to look down on ordinary people; but in the words of Edmund Burke, "the people have no interest in disorder. When they do wrong, it is their error and not their crime. But with the governing part of the state, it is far otherwise. They may certainly act ill by design, as well as by mistake" (1770: 8).

---

[165] See for instance (Lipson, 1949: 191).

Looking at the question logically rather than historically, we might expect consequences along the following lines – if and when negotiable debt is outlawed.

- Once the systemic robbery by banking and finance came to an end, working people would enjoy more of the fruits of their labours.

- A great deal more money would remain in circulation among 'ordinary people' instead of being drained off into tax havens.

- The amount of debt in the world would reduce dramatically if the money supply was no longer created as two reciprocal debts – one fake, the other real (see Chapter Three).

- It would be harder for governments to borrow because government debt would no longer be a valuable commodity (its ownership would no longer be transferable). Lending to the government would mean the lender doing without the money lent while it was in the hands of the government, as opposed to being given a valuable asset in return that can be used as collateral. Governments would no longer find it so easy to pile debt onto their citizenry.[166] (This obviously makes reform far more difficult to achieve!)

- Local communities would come economically to life, relieved of the continual drain on their activities by corporate ownership, which takes profits to distant tax-havens leaving debt behind.[167]

- Great corporations, which have grown fat on easy borrowing of credit-money and flourished as vehicles of remote ownership, would lose much of their advantage.

- Democracy would breathe new life. Here, historical examples shout out loud. When voters grow desperate but do not understand what is oppressing them, they vote for simplistic and destructive loudmouths to save them. These people bring not

---

[166] The question has been asked many times: when governments have the power to create money, why do they borrow money created by banks – at great expense to taxpayers, and at great profit to richer citizens? The standard economist's answer is that governments invariably create too much money. A better answer might be: when governments and plutocrats cooperate, power increases for both.

[167] An example of this at work in the present system: www.bit.ly/TPbr40

reform, but more exploitation and more destruction. Democracy must include 'the people' in decision-making, so that they understand the processes which dominate their lives. In the words of Lord Acton, "laws should be adapted to those who have the heaviest stake in the country, for whom misgovernment means not mortified pride or stinted luxury, but want and pain and degradation." (1913: 38)

- With democracy revitalised, aggressive and predatory politics would lose their attraction. Over the past century, we have been led into many evils: more potent weapons, planetary destruction, race hatreds, nationalisms, etc. 'The people' are often blamed for these evils, although the role of elites in determining them is no secret.[168]

- If the principle of negotiable debt were abandoned, ownership would become more direct, more involved, less remote. It is easy for remote owners to demand destructive practices when they never see the results. More owner-involvement would have dramatic consequences for nature and the environment. We could expect a reduction in the destructive exploitation of natural resources (see Chapter Seven). The natural world could begin to recover its health.

- We also might experience great changes in 'culture'. The creative role of culture is to enhance our understanding of the world, so that we may more intelligently determine our future. When culture is provided by commercial corporations, considerations of profit rule and culture becomes something quite different.

- War would surely not come to an end, but it would equally surely be lessened. Negotiable debt was developed for purposes of war-making, and economies based on credit-money depend on arms

---

[168] Democracy would be revitalised if a) jury-style selected committees were employed to make important political decisions after listening to arguments – just as juries do in courtrooms today; and b) representatives were chosen in popular assemblies at grass-roots level, where they would be known personally to those who choose them. Acton: "Where the extent of the electoral district obliges voters to vote for candidates who are unknown to them, the election is not free. It is managed by wire-pullers, and by party machinery, remote from the electors." (1907: 97). See also (Mosley, 2013: Ch 7).

production and war just to keep healthy (see Chapters Two, Seven and Eight).

- The power of great nations, armed with strong currencies and developed finance industries, to purchase the assets of weaker nations would diminish. Fewer people would be forced from their homes; traditional and more eco-friendly production practices might regain share in the markets.

- In this kind of revitalised world, public and private decision-making would focus more on issues of genuine significance and social concern such as climate change, the destruction of the environment, and the forced migrations of millions as their lands are purchased from under them and made uninhabitable by large-scale industrial farming and/or global warming.

- In a world of greater freedom, the guiding principles of our behaviour might change. The endless war in human hearts and minds, between the impulses to share, collaborate, cooperate on the one hand and on the other to grab, monopolise, and oppress might shift to a more healthy balance.[169]

Reform: How Should It Be Done?

There are three distinct approaches to reform. One is to fundamentally reform laws that make debt into a tradeable commodity. A second approach is to adjust the regulations so that the system can continue to operate, but within tighter constraints so that it's more stable. A third is to encourage alternative systems of currency, whether local credit systems or privately created systems such as 'bitcoin'. The second and third options could operate together. The first, implemented fully, would solve current problems and present a new (much simpler) set of problems, requiring new arrangements and procedures. It would make the other two approaches unnecessary and redundant.

---

[169] In Keynes' (1932) (somewhat hopeful and overstated) words, "The love of money as a possession – as distinguished from the love of money as a means to the enjoyments and realities of life – will be recognised for what it is, a somewhat disgusting morbidity, one of those semi-criminal, semi-pathological propensities which one hands over with a shudder to the specialists in mental disease."

Reforming the Laws

If we recognise that negotiable debt is the fundamental problem, reform becomes *in theory* relatively easy. Borrowing and lending would not be discouraged or forbidden – far from it. The change would be that only original lenders would be helped by the state to recover on a debt. Nations would simply reform their laws so that the buying and selling of debt is no longer supported.[170]

Only democratic pressure can bring about such reform. At present this seems far from likely. One problem is information. Public understanding of our money system is negligible. In an ever-worsening world, the public will continue to be attracted by unsavoury demagogues who promise change but who in reality deliver the same only worse.

If this kind of fundamental reform were undertaken, many questions would have to be answered. Here are a few of them: each question will be followed by a consideration of how it might be solved.

1. Should the law merely cease to support negotiable debt, or should the creation of negotiable debt be made a positively criminal activity? This question should be solved by a panel of people experienced in the multiple complexities of financial instruments: how they are used to make money, and to what extend they depend upon mutual trust or need the support of the law. Some are perhaps simply forms of gambling – 'zero sum games' in which gamblers win or lose without any impact on the wider community. Others are designed to increase asset prices for ordinary citizens, the profits going to those who trade in them. These are in the category of practices that rob others.

2. Could a nation 'go it alone' after reforming its laws? How would it interact with remaining systems, in which money continues to be created for predatory speculation? This seems to me, initially at least, the most difficult question. In his book *Sovereign Money* Joseph Huber says there should be no problem because "The final settlement of international payments is carried out in central bank

---

[170] Because every jurisdiction incorporates laws supporting the buying and selling of debt in a slightly different way, the details of legal reform would be different in each. Reform would emerge from accepting the principle and then applying it – much as slavery was abolished in most countries during the 19th century.

reserves anyway" (2016: 190). It seems to me, however, that a country might need to protect itself (for instance) from foreign banks dealing primarily in currencies where credit continues to be created as a weapon for predation.

3. Should there be an international currency, or unit of account, to intermediate trade between the world's currencies and to avoid the kind of currency war we see beginning between China and the USA? Keynes suggested such an arrangement after World War II (the 'Bancor') for slightly different reasons; but it was rejected.[171]

4. Should some sort of redistributive justice be undertaken, to redress the vast inequalities that have developed under our present system? As mentioned earlier, a precedent exists for this: the redistribution undertaken by the Allies in Germany after World War II. Vast fortunes had been accumulated by Nazi financiers and (above a certain level) these were forcibly reduced by over 90% after the war. Debts were also reduced by the same ratio. In addition, equal hand-outs of new money were given to all citizen-families. In addition to this vast burial of *domestic* debt, Germany's *foreign* debts were reduced by a similar percentage in the London Debt Agreement of 1953. These reductions were followed by the most dramatic economic recovery in recorded history – an economic 'miracle'.[172] The 'miracle' was really a predictable outcome of reducing inequality. After that, credit-creation was allowed to resume – and so, of course, inequality began to grow afresh. There had been no fundamental reform of the way money is created, only adjustment of some bad outcomes.

Today, perhaps for the first time in history, opportunities offer themselves for the development of extensive and just money systems in which money is property pure and simple, not negotiable debt. Digital payment systems and open ledgers make this a simple possibility: if today's money is digits, their transfer can be easily recorded and checked, their ownership acknowledged, and the process open to scrutiny. Cash, of course, would be interchangeable with digital holdings just as it is today. Lending and

---

[171]www.bit.ly/TPbr41

[172] Further reforms to reduce the wealth of great landowners and industrialists and 'equalize the burden' were, interestingly, abandoned. See (Kramer, 1991).

borrowing would still flourish, but debt would not be a commodity for speculation. Owing to the huge growth in internet activity and connectivity between people all over the world, opportunities for borrowing, lending and intermediation have grown exponentially over the past few decades. Crowd-sourcing or a more targeted approach is often the most attractive option when attempting to fund a project. A common anxiety is that under a reformed money system, governments would not be able to afford expensive new infrastructure projects. As mentioned in the Introduction, this should present no problem: financing such projects would come out of a) taxation, b) creation of new money to be spent into the economy and c) some borrowing. The result would be more democratic accountability and more transparency.

Fundamental monetary reform is inextricably tied up with political reform and with changes to power-relations within and between nations. These changes are also highly desirable in the interests of peace, justice and continued human life.

For instance: there is a feeling today among most people that globalisation should be less of a globalised kleptocracy and more a globalisation of justice in finance and trading. The founding principle of a state is to outlaw violence between its citizens; a 'new world order' should outlaw violence and robbery between nations. Efforts to do this over the last hundred years – for instance by the League of Nations and the United Nations – have been notably unsuccessful. Predatory credit, and the dependence of 'advanced' economies on arms production and war, have significantly contributed to this lack of success.

Money After Legal Reform

After reform, 'pure' money would behave mostly as it does now during buying, selling, and saving. It would behave very differently, however, for people who want to use it to make more. No longer could it be summoned from nowhere, like "spirits from the vasty deep".[173] No longer could money sit in a bank and earn interest. It would have to be lent for some purpose, and at some risk, before it yielded profit.[174]

---

[173] Glendower's phrase, in Shakespeare's *Henry IV Part One*.

[174] Today, banks pay depositors to let their money sit idle because it maintains their supply of 'reserves'. Without reserves, a bank cannot function in today's system, in which banks compete and cooperate (a monopoly banking system

On the other hand, transferring money between accounts at different banks would become relatively simple, because it would mean no more than transferring a number between ledgers; whereas now (in our two-tier system) it requires considerable ancillary activity involving reserve and central bank cooperation (Huber, 2016: 64-67).

The quantity of money in circulation would be steadier and more controllable. Money would no longer be cancelled when debts to banks were repaid: as a result, a great deal less would have to be created. In today's system, banks create and destroy money in continuous process; in addition, they create huge amounts of money when the mood is optimistic, then destroy huge amounts when pessimism takes over and loans are called in. One result of this, long-recognised, is that people over-commit themselves in optimistic boom-times then have to borrow to stay afloat when the boom turns sour, resulting in a huge increase in debts contracted by ordinary working citizens. 'Pure' money, on the other hand, would remain in circulation, and its amount would be controlled by public decision-making rather than corporate profiteers.

The profit in making new money would be 'one-off'. The profit in making 'pure' or permanent money – for instance, by coining gold, printing paper, gathering shells, growing tobacco, making holes in stones – is almost always one-off. When money is in lasting circulation, rulers have had to resort to desperate (and obvious) measures to profit a second time: in 1544, for instance, Henry VIII of England recalled all the coin and replaced it with coin made of cheaper metal.

Lending would involve human, and therefore moral, decision-making. A bank is legally obliged to create and lend money purely on the criterion of the profit it will yield;[175] humans, on the other hand, when lending money, act on all kinds of motives, and often profit is not even one of

---

would not need reserves). When debt owed by a bank (i.e. money) moves from one bank to another, 'reserve' moves to square the accounts. For a more detailed explanation, see (Huber, 2016: 70-1 [note16]). Sidney Homer noted in his classic tome on interest rates that once banks adopted fractional reserve, "instead of charging a fee for deposits, they began to pay interest on deposits" (1977: 148).

[175] This taps into a long debate about the amoral demands of corporations. Johannes Andreae (c.1270–1348) argued: How can you trust a creature that cannot be shamed or punished? F.W. Maitland (1850-1906) wished to write a book on 'the damnability of corporations' before his life was cut short.

them. For instance, moral disinclination would stop many from lending to develop new weapon systems or destroy woodlands.

The whole behaviour of money would be simpler to understand, not only for the public but also for politicians and workers in financial services. Money would work as it is *supposed* and mostly *understood* to work now: it would be a form of property that simply exists, and which is borrowed and lent by banks in much the same way as the rest of us borrow and lend.

Debt would be a private arrangement between borrower and lender, and the state would only help to recover a debt on behalf of the lender. An intermediary such as a bank would then do what most people think it does anyway: take in money as deposits and lend it out. Banks would no longer create the money they lend.

Reforming the Regulations

For obvious reasons, reform groups today tend to aim for changes in regulations rather than radical legal reform. For most, fundamental reform seems unrealistic or unachievable, given public fear of change, ignorance or indifference; for others, great concentrations of power seem necessary in our world of ceaseless aggression; perhaps for others, the workings of negotiable debt are not well understood.

Certainly, many who seek reform feel the best way to approach it is little-by-little, hoping to achieve what seems possible in the circumstances, not attempting to change the whole system all at once.

For many people, entrusting credit-creation to the state seems an attractive way forward despite historical examples provided by past governments with totalitarian power over negotiable debt. The idea is that in a genuine democracy, money would be created in a way beneficial to the majority. The reality, however, is that power tends to corrupt. The freedom of citizens grows ever more constrained as those in power consider themselves to have all the right ideas, instead of trusting the people to have better ideas among themselves.[176]

Whatever their approach, most reformers wish to make the money-creation system more just and less damaging. The kinds of change they

---

[176] Seen from another angle: "There is no doubt about the general character of the institution of property most friendly to freedom: it will be one which allows the widest distribution, and which discourages most effectively great and dangerous concentrations of this power" (Oakeshott, 1991: 393).

recommend can be summarised under various headings. These changes are recommended by different reformers, sometimes in varying combinations:

1. National banks of credit: the idea here is that state-owned banks would operate alongside (and in the same manner as) commercial banks; but instead of lending purely for profit, they would lend to projects with a social benefit. Banking profits would go to governments, thereby reducing taxation.[177]

2. 100% reserve. Here, banks would be obliged to keep as much value in reserve as they create in loans. If reserve was gold, this would mean keeping stocks of gold. Now that reserve is numbers loaned or sold by the government, it would mean governments lending the digits for 'reserve' and banks lending credit up to the level of that 'reserve'. Interest payments on the reserve would be a source of revenue for government. Many 100% reservists advocate going back to a reserve of gold. The aims here are financial and market stability, and less profit to creators of credit and those who exploit it.[178]

3. Free banking. Any private business would be free to create money; the marketplace would determine which currencies would be successful. Most free-bankers favour a gold reserve. Some free-bankers wish to see money loaned into existence; others would prefer that only pre-existing money be loaned. The common aim here is to reduce 'crony capitalism' – the damaging relationship between government patronage and wealth-creation, where those who succeed in finance have an open door to government.[179]

4. Sovereign Money. Here, the money supply is created by government not private banks; and as pure property not as credit (with the possible addition of a state bank issuing credit for public works). Non-credit money would be permanent, so more would only be created as the economy expanded (and conversely, cancelled if the economy contracts).[180]

---

[177] See for instance (Brown, 2013).

[178] The classic text is Irving Fisher (1935).

[179] White 1992; Selgin 1988.

[180] See (Dyson & Hodgson, 2016) and (Huber, 2016).

5.   An expanded role for community currencies, supplemented by credit-clearing circles based on actual goods and services. These systems already exist, but they have been side-lined into relative insignificance by the dominance of bank-created money. Essential here is the idea that credit should no longer be created out of nothing as interest-bearing debt.[181]

6.   Simple displacement of bank currency by externally-created digital currencies such as bitcoin, backed by the open ledger system of recording transactions ('blockchain').

7.   Changes to accounting rules, so that banks may no longer count debts to themselves as assets (McMillan, 2014).

8.   Access for everyone to accounts in reserve money (digital cash) at central bank accounts. Only banks and a few other financial institutions are currently allowed accounts at central banks. The Bank of England is researching the possibility of a central bank digital currency: in its own words, "a universally accessible and interest-bearing central bank liability, implemented via distributed ledgers, that competes with bank deposits as a medium of exchange."[182]

The two organisations that have serialised an earlier version of this book, Positive Money and the Cobden Centre, take different approaches to the problem of how to achieve a money supply that is more just, efficient and stable. Positive Money favours 1, 4 and 8 of these proposals; the Cobden Centre is keener on 2, 3 and 6. I believe both would look kindly on 5 and 7.

The main monetary re-think movement in the USA, Modern Monetary Theory, has many different proponents and versions. The main assertion seems to be that the government can create money and spend it: so long as spending goes toward expanding the economy, the excess will be mopped up and inflation will not occur. Also, that governments can finance a great deal of national debt by paying the interest with new money. "As long as there are enough workers and equipment to meet growing demand without igniting inflation, the government can spend what it needs to maintain employment and achieve goals such as halting climate change."[183]

---

[181] (Greco, 2001) and (Lietaer, 2013).

[182] Bank of England Staff Working Paper 605 (2016) proposes a form of 'digital cash' created as debt: downloadable at www.bit.ly/TPbr43

[183] www.bit.ly/TPbr44

MMT appears to ignore many facts: one, that the government in present circumstances creates only 'reserve' and cash, whereas most money that is spent into the economy is created by banks so a change in structure would be needed; also, that governments are not great at planning economic expansion: it is a free citizenry that are actively creative in this and other regards. In the opinion of many, it is not a movement for serious reform, more an impersonation of one.

Some Problems

One problem with these proposed reforms is their complexity: people need a good knowledge of today's financial system before they can grasp them. The simplicity of fundamental reform, and its thoroughness, are two features in its favour. Further, if banking regulations were to be changed without fundamental legal reform, would the myriad other tricks involving negotiable debt be allowed to continue? If not, how would they be stopped?

While debt remains negotiable, human ingenuity will invent new ways of conjuring value out of nothing. For instance, as banking became more regulated, the phenomenon of shadow banking emerged. "Banking that is not or only lightly regulated is often called shadow banking. Within a few decades, shadow banking became more important than traditional banking" (McMillan, 2014). These 'magic tricks' contribute nothing to the welfare of humanity: on the contrary, they do it immeasurable harm.

For these reasons, fundamental reform – an end to negotiable debt – seems to me the only possibility worth chasing with a chance of success.

The Transition to 'Sovereign' or 'Pure' Money

The transition from bank-created money to 'sovereign' or 'pure' money would involve a one-off re-definition of money units as units of pure property. Money would no longer be fantasy debt owed by a bank, it would be units of valuable property protected in law, supervised by rule of an authority, and recognised by citizens and the government.

Money, as it passes from hand to hand, would act in exactly the same way as it does today; only its beginning and its end would be different. Instead of being created at interest and for profit, and then destroyed again once profit is taken, it would circulate more-or-less permanently.

If the realistic proposals of Joseph Huber, The Cobden Centre and Positive Money were followed, present-day bank-created money would be re-defined as pure money.[184] It would no longer be debt from banks. These debts would simply disappear; but since they are fake debts, it would not be a windfall for banks, except that the corresponding debts from customers would remain. This would be manifestly unjust. One suggested solution to this injustice is that existing debts to banks should be re-allocated to governments. A solution along these lines is outlined by Joseph Huber: as debts are repaid to commercial banks, the money would be passed on to ownership by the central bank (2016: 172).

Many economists insist that a transition would present few problems. If troubles do arise (perhaps along the lines of those listed above) a number of emergency techniques could be put into operation. Some have been put to partial and preliminary test in today's chaotic financial world: examples are capital controls; price and wage controls; restrictions on currency movements, purchases and exchange, and the use of an intermediate and neutral international 'world' currency or unit of account.

Creation and Destruction of Money Under the New System

It has long been recognised that the justice system should be kept separate from the selfish short-term interests and vagaries of political power. The same should surely be true for the creation of the money supply.

This is why, many reformers have proposed an independent authority to decide how much money should be created or destroyed. The most detailed modern recommendation I know of is that of Henry Simons.[185] The authority's decisions would be determined by a single objective: to steady the value of money. The idea is not at all unrealistic. For instance, in England today the Monetary Policy Committee acts responsibly and authoritatively – but to a different script. Under the new script, created money would not be rented out as debt but spent into the economy.

The reason for aiming at a steady value for money is that it favours neither borrowers nor lenders, producers nor consumers, workers nor

---

[184] Cobden Centre: (Huerta De Soto, 2006: Ch 9). Positive Money: (Dyson, Hodgson & van Lerven, 2016, Ch 5). Joseph Huber: (Huber, 2016: 170-4).

[185] "The importance of rules, and of focussing democratic discussion on general principles of policy, calls for emphasis… only by adherence to wise rules of action can we escape a political opportunism which jeopardizes and destroys what we wish most to protect and to preserve." (Simons, 1948: 202). See also (Robertson, 1959: Vol III Ch 2).

capitalists; it is even-handed and just.[186] When there is a need for *more* money – perhaps because the economy has grown – the authority would tell the government to create and spend a certain amount of money into the economy – thereby reducing the need for taxation.

If, on the other hand, a tendency to inflation is detected, money would be 'retired'. The authority would command the government to destroy a certain amount of money gained by taxation.

No Reform?

Many who argue that reform is undesirable say that conflict, robbery and warfare are an inherent part of human behaviour and high concentrations of power are necessary to protect nations from each other. This is similar to the US 'gun lobby' argument: that individuals need sophisticated weaponry to defend themselves. Both arguments are rooted in the self-interest of those who make them. The answer is that an equitable and effective rule of law may preserve peace so we can get on with living in conditions of freedom. The challenge is to build effective, equitable systems of law locally, nationally and internationally and thereby create a world community in which robbery, deceit and war are minimised. To give up on this is to accept savagery.

How Possible is Reform?

There is no point belittling the problem. We live in a system that's tailor-made to end civilisation as we know it: the system allocates enormous concentrations of power, which are an invitation to abuse – and are actually an abuse in themselves.

At present, there seems little hope for reform. No powerful interest group wants reform, even though debt and inter-related problems have been growing faster than ever.[187] Elites chase more money and more power – and bank-money fuels the chase.[188]

---

[186] When the value of money alters, some win and some lose. If money goes down in value (inflation), debtors win. If it goes up in value (deflation), creditors win.

[187] www.bit.ly/TPbr45

[188] Bad conscience gives rise to a culture of escapism and/or negativity.

Many people are frightened of rocking the boat; others feel helpless or excluded, and still others do not want to think about such complexity. In addition, most people are fully engaged with making ends meet.

The Roman Empire collapsed because no simple ideology of reform developed to reverse its drift to self-destruction. Circumstances – ever-growing inequality, poverty and oppression for the masses – got worse and worse but "a unified revolutionary movement was never able to develop" (Alföldy, 1988). A similar situation exists today: a smattering of would-be reformers, powerless to do anything, is in any case divided over what should be done; and meanwhile, inequality grows.

Hopeful Signs

There are, however, some hopeful signs and possibilities emerging. On the one hand, more and more people are becoming aware that the system is kleptocratic. Banks and finance interests are becoming increasingly – and more obviously – toxic drivers of inequality. Backed by state guarantees, they behave ever more greedily and irresponsibly. They invest more in asset-speculation than in productive investment. Their insolvency is becoming more obvious, more well-known, and more of a threat to the rest of us.

People in the banking world itself are becoming aware that the system needs reforming; and that their once-respected status in the world has changed. Recently I questioned a leading banking lawyer whether he thought banking law should be reformed. "I certainly do!" he said. I asked if he agreed with my definition of bank-created money: "the greatest system of kleptocracy ever invented and foisted on the human race". "Do you know," he said, "that is exactly how I think of it!"

His opinion corresponds with the opinions of many respected historical figures: for instance, 2nd and 3rd American Presidents, John Adams and Thomas Jefferson (some of their opinions are quoted in Chapter Six). The insights of people like Jefferson and Adams have long been ignored: maybe it is time now for them at last to take centre stage. Their predictions have taken many years to come true, but today they are undeniably valid.

Today, possibilities that could lead towards major reform are happening all by themselves. For instance, payment systems (such as Paypal and Google Pay) outside banks are proliferating; but they have to use money created by banks because bank-money dominates the world.

This domination is not an outcome of the market-place: banks enjoy unfair advantages. Besides their legal advantages, which make them able to create money as fake debt, banks are supported by huge and expensive state apparatuses. Licensing restricts their number; regulation prevents them from self-destructing; corporate status protects shareholders from possible bad outcomes of trading on a "mass of current obligations and a shoestring of equity" (Simons, 1948: 198) and government support underwrites their losses. In other words, huge amounts of tax-payers' money are used to support banks and the system they feed.

As already mentioned, because of these advantages, banks can out-compete other kinds of money by sharing some profits with customers. They provide some services free of charge (for instance, cash machines) and pay for others (such as storing money long-term). Alternative currencies cannot compete in the market-place with the privileges and advantages of banks.[189]

Truths are emerging through the cracks in the system: for instance, central banks are beginning to distance themselves from the results of money-creation by emphasising that *they* do not create the money supply: commercial banks do.[190]

One possible route towards reform would be for central banks – even one central bank – to issue 'pure' money, and to allow ordinary people to hold accounts. The Bank of England's intention to give 'non-bank Payments Service Providers' access to its settlement system perhaps signifies a move in this direction (until now only banks have hitherto had access to this, the central payment ledger of the British economy).[191]

A pioneering example of a new money system, excluding and avoiding bank-created money completely and not created as 'credit', might open the eyes of many to the possibilities of a more just and prosperous world.

And that would surely be a good thing.

---

[189] Privately-created digital currencies such as bitcoin are, at present, mostly vehicles for speculation.

[190] The German central bank has acknowledged this recently (to declare itself not responsible for creating too much money): www.bit.ly/TPbr46.

[191] www.bit.ly/TPbr47

Appendix 1

Sir John Holt's remarks on promissory notes

"Buller v. Crips, 6 Mod. 29, was an action upon a note by the indorsee against the maker; and the plaintiff declared upon the custom of merchants as upon a bill of exchange. Upon a motion in arrest of judgment, Holt, C. J. said : "The notes in question are only an invention of the goldsmiths in Lombard Street, who had a mind to make a law to bind all those that did deal with them; and sure to allow such a note to carry any lien with it were to turn a piece of paper, which is in law but evidence of a parol contract, into a specialty; and besides, it would empower one to assign that to another which he could not have himself; for since he to whom this note was made could not have this action, how can his assignee have it? And these notes are not in the nature of bills of exchange; for the reason of the custom of bills of exchange is for the expedition of trade and its safety; and likewise it hinders the exportation of money out of the realm.""

Appendix 2

Extract from The Promissory Notes Act, 1704

"An act for giving like remedy upon promissory notes, as is now used upon bills of exchange, and for the better payment of inland bills of exchange. Whereas it hath been held, that notes in writing, signed by the party who makes the same, whereby such party promises to pay unto any other person, or his order, any sum of money therein mentioned, are not assignable or indorsible over, within the custom of merchants, to any other person; and that such person to whom the sum of money mentioned in such note is payable, cannot maintain an action, by the custom of merchants, against the person who first made and signed the same; and that any person to whom such note shall be assigned, indorsed, or made payable, could not, within the said custom of merchants, maintain any action upon such note against the person who first drew and signed the same: therefore to the intent to encourage trade and commerce, which will be much advanced, if such notes shall have the same effect as inland bills of exchange, and shall be negotiated in like manner; be it enacted by the Queen's most excellent majesty, by and with the advice and consent of the lords spiritual and temporal, and commons, in this present parliament assembled, and by the authority of the same, that all notes in writing, that after the first day of May, in the year of our Lord, one thousand seven hundred and five, shall be made and signed by any person or persons, body politick, or corporate, or by the servant or agent of any corporation, banker, goldsmith, merchant, or trader, who is usually intrusted by him, her or them, to sign such promissory notes for him, her, or them, whereby such person or persons, body politick and corporate, his, her, or their servant or agent, as aforesaid, doth or shall promise to pay to any other person or persons, body politick and corporate, his, her or their order, or unto bearer, any sum of money mentioned in such note, shall be taken and construed to be, by virtue thereof, due and payable to any such person or persons, body politick and corporate, to whom the same is made payable; and also every such note payable to any person or persons, body politick and corporate, his, her, or their order, shall be assignable or indorsible over, in the same manner as inland bills of exchange are or may be, according to the custom of merchants."

(Quoted in Coquillette, 1988: 278-9)

Bibliography

Acton, John Dahlberg, Lord (1877) 'The History of Freedom in Christianity', Internet Archive (download)

_____ (1906) *Lectures in Modern History*, Internet Archive (download)

_____ (1907) *The History of Freedom and Other Essays*, Macmillan. Available at libertyfund.org

_____ (1913) *Letters to Mary Gladstone*, Macmillan. Available at libertyfund.org

Adams, Charles (1992) For *Good and Evil: Impact of Taxes Upon the Course of Civilization*, Madison Books

Ahamed, Liaquat (2009) *Lords of Finance: 1929, The Great Depression - and the Bankers Who Broke the World*, William Heinemann

Alföldy, Geza (1988) *The Social History of Rome*, Johns Hopkins University Press

Allais, Maurice (1987) 'The Credit Mechanism and its Implications' in *Arrow and the Foundations of the Theory of Economic Policy*, ed. George R. Feiwel, Palgrave Macmillan

Allais, Maurice (1999) *La Crise Mondiale d'Aujourd'hui. Pour de profondes réformes des institutions financières et monétaires*, Clément Juglar

Allchin, Joseph (2016) 'Bangladesh's Other Banking Scam', *New York Times*, 11 April

Amemiya, Takeshi, (2007) *Economy and Economics of Ancient Greece*, Routledge

Anderson, Benjamin (1980) *Economics and the Public Welfare*, Liberty Fund

Anderson, Judith H. (2005) *Translating Investments: Metaphor and the Dynamics of Cultural Change in Tudor-Stuart England*, Fordham University Press

Andreau, Jean (1999) *Banking and Business in the Roman World*, Cambridge University Press

Anon, (1841) 'Banking and Paper Money' in *The Southern Magazine and Monthly Review*, No. 1

_____ (2013a) *Civil Affairs Handbook, Germany, Section 4: Government Finance*, BiblioGov

_____ (2013b) *Civil Affairs Handbook, Germany, Section 5: Money and Banking*, BiblioGov

_____ (2013c) *Civil Affairs Handbook, Germany, Section 5: Money and Banking Part Two*, BiblioGov

Arendt, Hannah (1972) *Crises of the Republic: Lying in Politics; Civil Disobedience; On Violence; Thoughts on Politics and Revolution*, Harcourt

Ashby, J. F. (1934) *The Story of the Banks*, Hutchinson

Ashley, Maurice (1982) *The People of England: A Short Social and Economic History*, Weidenfeld and Nicolson

Ashley, Sir William (1914/2009) *The Economic Organisation of England*, Cornell

_____ (2016) *An Introduction to English Economic History and Theory*, Palala

Ashton, T.S. & Sayers, R.S. (1964) *Papers in English Monetary History*, Clarendon Press

Ashworth, William (2003) *Customs and Excise: trade, production and consumption in England 1640-1845*, Oxford University Press

Bachofen, Johann Jakob (1967) *Myth, Religion, and Mother Right: Selected writings of J. J. Bachofen*, Trans. Ralph Manheim, Princeton Univ. Press

Bacque, James (1998) *Crimes and Mercies*, Time Warner Paperbacks

Bagehot, Walter (1873) *Lombard Street: A Description of the Money Market*, Henry S. King

Baird, Henry Carey (1875) *Inflated Bank Credit*, Internet Archive (download)

Bank of England (2014) 'Money in the modern economy: an introduction' and 'Money creation in the modern economy' in *Quarterly Bulletin 2014 Q1*

Baran, P. A. & Sweezy, P. M. (1969) *Monopoly Capital*, Monthly Review Press

Baran, P. A. (1968) *The Political Economy of Growth*, Monthly Review Press

Barbour, Violet. (1950) *Capitalism in Amsterdam in the Seventeenth Century*, John Hopkins University Press

Barkai, Avraham (1990) *Nazi Economics*, Yale University Press

Barker, E. (1948) *The Politics of Aristotle*, Oxford University Press

Bartlett, Bruce (1994) 'How Excessive Government Killed Ancient Rome' in *Cato Journal*

Baster, A.S.J. (1977) *The International Banks*, Arno Press

Bastiat, Frederic (2007) *The Bastiat Collection*, Ludwig von Mises Inst., online

Bauer, P.T. (1981) *Equality, the Third World and Economic Delusion*, Littlehampton Book Services

_____ (1986) *Reality and Rhetoric: Studies in the Economics of Development*, Harvard University Press

_____ (2004) *From Subsistence to Exchange and Other Essays*, Princeton University Press

Baumol, William J., Litan, Robert E. and Schramm, Carl J. (2009) *Good Capitalism, Bad Capitalism, and the Economics of Growth and Prosperity*, Yale University Press

Beard, Mary (2012) 'Modern tax farming and the Roman dangers of private enterprise' in *The Times Literary Supplement*, 15 August

Behrens, Kathryn (1923) *Paper Money in Maryland 1727-1789*, Questia online

Beinhocker, Eric (2007) *The Origin of Wealth: Evolution, Complexity, and the Radical Remaking of Economics*, Random House Business

Benham, Frederic (1944) *Economics*, Pitman

Berkeley, Bishop (1735) *The Querist*, John Hopkins Press, Internet Archive (download)

Berkey, William A. (2006) *The Money Question. The legal tender paper monetary system of the United States.* Michigan Historical Reprint Series

Berlin, Isaiah (1995) *Karl Marx*, Fontana

Berman, Harold Joseph, (1983) *Law and Revolution: The formation of the Western legal tradition*, Harvard University Press

_____ (2004) *Law and Revolution. Vol. 2: The impact of the Protestant Reformation on the Western legal tradition*, Belknap

Birks, Peter (2005) *Unjust Enrichment*, Clarendon Press

Bisschop, Willem Roosegaarde (1968) *The Rise of the London Money Market, 1640-1826*, Cass

Blackstone, W. (1765) *Commentaries, Books 1-4.* Internet Archive (download)

Blaug, Mark (ed., 1991) *Pre-Classical Economists. Vol.1, Charles Davenant (1656-1714) and William Petty (1623-1687)*, Elgar

Blum, William (1998) *Killing Hope: US Military and CIA Interventions Since World War Two*, Black Rose Books

Bolingbroke, Henry St. John (1749) *The Idea of a Patriot King*

Bonnyman, Brian (2014) *The Third Duke of Buccleuch and Adam Smith*, Edinburgh University Press

Bordo, Michael D. & White, Eugene N. (1991) 'A Tale of Two Currencies: British and French Finance During the Napoleonic Wars' in *The Journal of Economic History*, Vol. 51, No. 2

Borio, C. and Disyatat, P. 'Global imbalances and the financial crisis: Link or no link?' *Bank for International Settlements, Working Paper No 346.* Available online

Bourne, Randolph Silliman (1999) *War and the Intellectuals: Collected Essays, 1915-1919*, Hackett

Bowden, Witt (2012) *An Economic History of Europe since 1750*, Literary Licensing

Brantlinger, Patrick (1996) *Fictions of State: Culture and Credit in Britain, 1694-1994*, Cornell University Press

Brewer, John (2014) *The Sinews of Power: War, Money and the English State, 1688-1783*, Routledge

Broughton, John (1705) *Remarks Upon the Bank of England*, Internet Archive (download)

_____ (1707) *An Essay Upon The National Credit of England*, Internet Archive (download)

Brown, Ellen (2013) *The Public Bank Solution: From Austerity to Prosperity*, Third Millennium

Bryan, Frank M. (2004) *Real Democracy: The New England Town Meeting and How it Works*, University of Chicago Press

Buist, M.G. (1977) 'The Sinews of War: the role of Dutch finance in European politics c. 1750-1815' in *Britain and the Netherlands* ed. Duke & Tamse, Martinus Nijhoff

Burckhardt, Jacob (1963) *The Greeks and Greek Civilization*, Harper Collins

_____ (1964) *History of Greek Culture*, Constable

Burgis, Tom (2015) *The Looting Machine: Warlords, Tycoons, Smugglers and the Systematic Theft of Africa's Wealth*, Harper Collins

Burke, Edmund (1770) *Thoughts on the Cause of the Present Discontents*, Dodsley

Cam, Helen (1967) *England Before Elizabeth*, Hutchinson

Cambridge Modern History, Volume 5 (1908) Cambridge University Press

Cameron, Rondo (1967) *Banking in the Early Stages of Industrialization: A Study in Comparative Economic History*, Oxford University Press

Cantillon, Richard (1755) *Essay on Economic Theory*, Internet Archive (download)

Cappon, Lester (ed.) (2008) *The Adams-Jefferson Letters: The Complete Correspondence Between Thomas Jefferson and Abigail and John Adams*

Carey, Daniel & Finlay, Christopher (eds.) (2011) *The Empire of Credit: The financial revolution in Britain, Ireland and America, 1688-1815*, Irish Academic Press

Carswell, John (1961) *The South Sea Bubble*, Cresset Press

Carter, Alice Clare (1974) *Getting, Spending and Investing in Early Modern Times: Essays on Dutch, English and Huguenot Economic History*, K.Van Gorcum

Carus-Wilson, E. M. (ed) (1966) *Essays in Economic History*, Edward Arnold

Cary, John (1696) *An Essay on the Coyn and Credit of England*, Internet Archive (download)

Chaudhuri, Sushil (2008) *Cashless Payments and Transactions from the Antiquity to 1914*, Franz Steiner Verlag

Checkland, S. G. (1975) *Scottish Banking: A History, 1695-1973*, HarperCollins

Chitty, Joseph (1834) *A Practical Treatise on Bills of Exchange*, Internet Archive (download)

Chomsky, Noam (1998) *Profit over People: Neoliberalism and the Global Order*, Seven Stories

Christophers, Brett (ed.) (2017) *Money and Finance After the Crisis: Critical Thinking for Uncertain Times* Antipode Book Series

Cipolla, C.M. (1975) *The Fontana Economic History of Europe - The Industrial Revolution*, Fontana

Clapham, Sir John (1944) *The Bank of England: A History: Volumes I and II*, Cambridge University Press

Clark, G.N. (1947) *The Wealth of England from 1496 to 1760*, Oxford University Press

_____ (1963) *The Later Stuarts 1660-1714*, Oxford University Press

Clarke, M. V. (1926) *The Medieval City State*, Routledge

_____ (1936) *Medieval Representation and Consent*, Longmans, Green & Co.

Cobb, Richard & Jones, Colin (1988) *The French Revolution: Voices from a Momentous Epoch*, Simon & Schuster

Coffey, Luke (2016) 'A Tangled Web of Corruption is Strangling Moldova', Nationalinterest.org, August 29

Cohan, William D. (2017) *Why Wall Street Matters*, Penguin

Cohen, Edward (1997) *Athenian Economy and Society: A Banking Perspective*, Princeton University Press

Cole, G.D.H. (1953) *History of Socialist Thought v. 1: The Forerunners, 1789-1850*, Macmillan

_____ (1954) *History of Socialist Thought v. 2: Marxism and Anarchism 1850-1890*, Macmillan

Collins, Andrew and Walsh, John (2014) 'Fractional Reserve Banking in the Roman Republic and Empire' in *Ancient Society* 44:179-212

Commons, John R. (1924) *Legal Foundations of Capitalism*, Macmillan

Coquillette, Daniel R. (1988) *The Civilian Writers of Doctors' Commons*, Duncker & Humblot

_____ (2007) *Lawyers and Fundamental Moral Responsibility: Materials*, Anderson

Cottrell, P.L. (1974) *Money and Banking in England: Development of the Banking System, 1694-1914*, David & Charles

Cranch, William (1812) *Reports of Cases Argued and Adjudged in the Supreme Court of the United States: Volume 1*, Internet Archive (download)

Crawford, Alan Pell (2008) *Twilight at Monticello: The Final Years of Thomas Jefferson*, Random House

Creutz, Helmut (2010) *The Money Syndrome*, Upfront Publishing

Crick, F.W. (1927) 'The Genesis of Bank Deposits' *Economica* 7

Crockett, Andrew (1981) *Money: Theory, Policy and Institutions*, Nelson

Crosland, C.A.R. (1957) *The Future of Socialism*, Jonathan Cape

Crowther, Geoffrey (1940) *An Outline of Money*, Thomas Nelson

Darwin, Charles (1875) *The Descent of Man*, Internet Archive (download)

Davies, Glyn (2010) *History of Money: From Ancient Times to the Present Day*, University of Wales

Dawisha, Karen (2015) *Putin's Kleptocracy: Who Owns Russia?*, Simon & Schuster

Defoe**Error! Bookmark not defined.**, Daniel (1702) *The Original Power of the Collective Body of the People of England Examined and Asserted*, Google Books (download)

De Roover, Raymond (1949) *Gresham on Foreign Exchange: An Essay on Early English mercantilism with the Text of Sir Thomas Gresham's Memorandum, For the Understanding of the Exchange*, Harvard University Press

_____ (1953) *L'Evolution de la Lettre de Change: XIVe-XVIIIe siècles*, Armand Colin

_____ (1963) Review of 'Banking and Finance among Jews in Renaissance Italy: A Critical Edition of "The Eternal Life" by Yehiel Nissim da Pisa' in *The Business History Review*

_____ (1974) *The Rise and Decline of the Medici Bank, 1397-1494*, Harvard University Press

_____ (1975) *Business, Banking, and Economic Thought in Late Medieval and Early Modern Europe*, University of Chicago Press

_____ (2007) *Money, Banking and Credit in Mediaeval Bruges – Italian Merchant Bankers, Lombards and Money Changers*, Rinsland Press

Dickinson, H.T. (1977) *Liberty and Property: Political Ideology in 18th Century Britain*, University Paperbacks

Dickson, P.G.M. (1967) *The Financial Revolution in England, 1688-1756: A Study in the Development of Public Credit*, Macmillan

Dowd, Kevin (2010) *The Alchemists of Loss: How Modern Finance and Government Intervention Crashed the Financial System*, Wiley

Duffy, Dr Cian (2011) *Cultures of the Sublime: Selected Readings, 1750-1830*, Palgrave

Dunbar, C. F. (1887) 'Deposits as Currency' in *Quarterly Journal of Economics*

_____ (1893) *The Theory and History of Banking*, Internet Archive download

_____ (1904) *Economic Essays*, Internet Archive (download)

Dyson, Ben & Hodgson, Graham (2016) *Digital Cash: Why Central Banks Should Start Issuing Electronic Money*, Positive Money

Dyson, Ben, Hodgson, Graham & van Lerven, Frank (2016) *Sovereign Money: An Introduction*, Positive Money (downloadable)

Edwards, David C. (2005) *Guardians of Power: The Myth of the Liberal Media*, Pluto Press

Edwards, George W. (2014) *The Evolution of Finance Capitalism*, Martino Fine Books

Einzig, Paul (1949) *Primitive Money in its Ethnological, Historical and Economic Aspects*, Eyre & Spottiswoode

Ellinger, E. P. (2006) *Ellinger's Modern Banking Law*, Oxford University Press

Feavearyear, Sir A. (1963) *The Pound Sterling*, Oxford University Press

Feiwel, George R. (ed.) (2014) *Arrow and the Foundations of the Theory of Economic Policy*, Palgrave Macmillan

Ferguson, Niall (2008) *The Ascent of Money: A Financial History of the World*, Allen Lane

Fetter, Frank W. (1965) *The Development of British Monetary Orthodoxy 1797-1875*, Harvard University Press

Fisher, Irving et al. (1939) *A Program for Monetary Reform*, Internet Archive (download)

Fisher, Irving (1935) *100% Money*. www.bit.ly/TPbr42

Fitzmaurice, Lord Edmond (1895) *The Life of Sir William Petty*, John Murray

Forman, Martin (1976) *Factoring and Finance*, Heinemann

Foroohar, Rana (2017) *Makers and Takers: How Wall Street Destroyed Main Street*, Crown Vintage

Franklin, Benjamin (1729) 'A Modest Inquiry into the Nature and Necessity of a Paper Currency'

_____ (1767) *Remarks and Facts Concerning American Paper Money*, Internet Archive (download)

_____ (1905-7) *Writings Vols I-X*, Internet Archive (download)

_____ (2008) *Autobiography and Other Writings*, Oxford University Press

Freire, Paulo (2017) *Pedagogy of the Oppressed*, Penguin

Frey, Donald E. (2010) *America's Economic Moralists: A History of Rival Ethics and Economics*, State University of New York Press

Friedman, Milton (1948) 'A Monetary and Fiscal Framework for Economic Stability' in *The American Economic Review*, Vol. 38, No. 3

Frisby, Dominic (2014) *Bitcoin: The Future of Money?*, Unbound

Fuller, Roslyn (2015) *Beasts and Gods: How Democracy Changed its Meaning and Lost its Purpose*, Zed Books

Galbraith, J. K. (1989) *Money: Whence it Came, Where it Went*, Pelican Books

_____ (2009) *The Economics of Innocent Fraud: Truth for Our Time*, Penguin

Garner, Bryan (2011) *Black's Law Dictionary*, West Publishing Company

Geva, Benjamin (2011) *The Payment Order of Antiquity and the Middle Ages*, Hart Publishing

Gillespie, John & Zweig, David (2011) *Money for Nothing: How CEOs and Boards Are Bankrupting America*, Free Press

Gilliland, C. L. C. (1975) *The Stone Money of Yap: A Numismatic Survey*, Smithsonian

Gimbutas, Marija (1991) *The Civilization of the Goddess: The World of Old Europe*, HarperSanFrancisco

Goettner-Abendroth, Heide (2012) *Matriarchal Societies: Studies on Indigenous Cultures Across the Globe*, Peter Lang

Goetzmann, William N. & Rouwenhorst, K. Geert (eds.) (2004) *The Origins of Value: The Financial Innovations that Created Modern Capital Markets*, Oxford University Press

Gouge, William M. (1833) *A Short History of Paper Money and Banking in The United States, To Which is Prefixed an Inquiry into The Principles of the System*, Internet Archive (download)

_____ (1837) *An Inquiry into the Expediency of Dispensing with Bank Agency and Bank Paper*, Internet Archive (download)

_____ (1843a) 'Banking as it ought to be' in *The United States Magazine and Democratic Review*

_____ (1843b) 'Commercial Banking' in *Hunt's Merchants' Magazine Vol. 8*, Internet Archive (download)

_____ (2011) *The Journal Of Banking From July 1841 To July 1842: Containing Essays On Various Questions Relating To Banking And Currency*, Nabu Press

Graeber, David (2011) *Debt: The First 5,000 Years*, Melville House

Graham, Frank D. (1930) *Exchange, Prices, and Production in Hyper-Inflation Germany 1920-1923*, Russell & Russell

_____ (1936a) *Money: What it Is and What it Does*, Newson & Company

_____ (1936b) 'Partial Reserve Money and the 100 Per Cent Proposal' in *The American Economic Review Vol. 26*

_____ (1942a) *Economic Preparation and Conduct of War under the Nazi Regime*, Historical Division, War Department

_____ (1942b) *Social Goals and Economic Institutions*, Princeton Univ. Press

Graham, Frank D. *The Theory of International Values*, Princeton Univ. Press

Gray, Alexander (1931) *The Development of Economic Doctrine*, Longman

Greco, Thomas (2001) *Money: Understanding and Creating Alternatives to Legal Tender*, Chelsea Green

Green, Edwin: (1989) *Banking, an Illustrated History*, Phaidon

Grice-Hutchinson, Marjorie (1978) *Early Economic Thought in Spain, 1177-1740*, Allen and Unwin

Grubb, Farley (2007) *Benjamin Franklin and the Birth of a Paper Money Economy*, downloadable at modernmoneynetwork.org

Guizot, Francois (2013) *History of Civilization in Europe*, Liberty Fund

Hagemann, Harald, L. (2010) *Albert Hahn's Economic Theory of Bank Credit*, Vienna University of Economics and Business

Hahn, Lucien A. (2012) *The Economics of Illusion*, New York Inst. of Finance

Hamilton, Alexander (1904) *Works*, ed. Lodge 10 vols., Internet Archive (download)

Hammond, Bray (1936) 'Free Banks and Corporations: The New York Free Banking Act of 1838' in *Journal of Political Economy*, Vol. 44, No. 2

_____ (1947) 'Jackson, Biddle, and the Bank of the United States' in *The Journal of Economic History* Vol. 7, no 1

_____ (1957) *Banks and Politics in America: From the Revolution to the Civil War*, Princeton University Press

_____ (2016) *Sovereignty and an Empty Purse – Banks and Politics in the Civil War*, Princeton University Press

Hammond, J.L. & Hammond, Barbara (1917) *The Town Labourer*, Longman

_____ (1987) *The Village Labourer, 1760-1832*, Sutton Publishing

Hampsher-Monk, Iain (1993) *A History of Modern Political Thought: Major Political Thinkers from Hobbes to Marx*, Wiley-Blackwell

Hansen, M. H. (2014) *Reflections on Aristotle's Politics*, Museum Tusculanum

Harris, W. V. (ed., 2008) *The Monetary Systems of the Greeks and Romans*, Oxford University Press

Harvey, David (2011) *The Enigma of Capital: And the Crises of Capitalism*, Profile Books

Heckscher, Eli F. (1955) *Mercantilism Vols One & Two*, Allen & Unwin

Helm, June (ed.) (1965) *Essays in Economic Anthropology*, American Ethnological Society

Henderson, (1983) *Friedrich List: Economist and Visionary*, Routledge

Herzog, W.R. (1994) *Parables as Subversive Speech: Jesus as Pedagogue of the Oppressed*, Westminster John Knox Press

Hibbert, Christopher (1982) *The French Revolution*, Penguin

Hixson, William F (1991) *A Matter of Interest: Re-examining Money, Debt, and Real Economic Growth*, Praeger

_____ (1997) *It's Your Money*, Comer

_____ (2005a) *What's the Difference Between Bankers and Counterfeiters?* E-BookTime

_____ (2005b) *Triumph of the Bankers*, E-BookTime

Hodgson, Graham (2013) *Banking, Finance and Income Inequality*, Positive Money

Hogeland, William (2012) *Founding Finance: How Debt, Speculation, Foreclosures, Protests, and Crackdowns Made Us a Nation*, University of Texas Press

Holden, J. Milnes (1955) *The History of Negotiable Instruments in English Law*, University of London Press

Holdsworth, William Searle, (1920) 'The History of the Treatment of "Choses" in Action by the Common Law' in *Harvard Law Review*

_____ (1925) *History of English Law Vol.8*, Internet Archive (download)

_____ (1946) *Essays in Law and History*, Clarendon Press

Hollis, Christopher (2015) *The Two Nations: A Financial Study of English History*, Routledge

Holloway Edward (1981) *How Guernsey Beat The Bankers*, Toucan

Homer, Sidney (1986) *History of Interest Rates*, Rutgers University Press

Horsefield, J. Keith, (1944) 'The Origins of the Bank Charter Act, 1844' in *Economica*

_____ (1960) *British Monetary Experiments 1650-1710*, Harvard Univ. Press

Huber, Joseph (2016) *Sovereign Money: Beyond Reserve Banking*, Palgrave Macmillan

Hudson, Michael (2002) *Debt and Economic Renewal in the Ancient Near East*, Capital Decisions

_____ (2011) 'Debt Slavery: Why It Destroyed Rome And Why it Will Destroy Us Unless It's Stopped' in *Counterpunch*

_____ (2015a) *Finance as Warfare*, College Publications

_____ (2015b) *Killing the Host*, Islet

_____ (2018) *...and forgive them their debts: Lending, Foreclosure and Redemption from Bronze Age Finance to the Jubilee Year*, Islet

Huerta de Soto, Jesus (2006) *Money, Bank Credit and Economic Cycles*, Ludwig von Mises Institute

Hume, David (1754) 'Of Public Credit' in *Essays and Treatises*, Internet Archive (download)

Humphrey, Thomas M. (1987) 'The Theory Of Multiple Expansion Of Deposits: What It Is And Whence It Came' in *Economic Review*. Available online at the Federal Bank of Richmond website

Hunt, Bishop Carleton (1969), *Russell & The Development of the Business Corporation in England, 1800-1867*

Hutchison, T. W. (1988) *Before Adam Smith: the emergence of political economy, 1662-1776*, B. Blackwell

IIF (Institute of International Finance) (2018), 'Global Debt Monitor: Hidden vulnerabilities', www.bit.ly/TPbr22

J.R. (1676) *The Mystery of the New-fashioned Goldsmiths or Bankers, their rise, growth, ... and decay*, Google Books (download)

Jackson, Andrew & Dyson, Ben (2013) *Modernising Money: Why Our Monetary System is Broken and How it Can be Fixed*, Positive Money

Janeway, Eliot (1968) *Economics of Crisis*, Weybright and Talley

Jefferson, Thomas (1999) *Political Writings*, Cambridge University Press

Jenks, Leland H. (1927) *Migration of British Capital to 1875*, Internet Archive (download)

Johnson, Brian (1970) *The Politics of Money*, John Murray

Johnson, Cuthbert William (1839) *The Law of Bills of Exchange, Promissory Notes, Checks, &c.*, Internet Archive (download)

Johnson, Douglas (1970) *The French Revolution (Pictorial Sources)*, Wayland

Johnson, Edgar Augustus Jerome (1937) *Predecessors of Adam Smith: the growth of British economic thought*, Prentice Hal

Johnson, Paul (2010) *Making the Market: Victorian Origins of Corporate Capitalism*, Cambridge University Press

Jones, A.H.M. (1968) *A History of Rome Through the Fifth Century. Vol. 1, The Republic*, Macmillan

_____ (1974) *The Roman economy: studies in ancient economic and administrative history*, Blackwell

Jones, Orville Davis (1888) *Principles of Moral and Political Economy*, Library of Congress

Jowett, Benjamin (1885) *The Politics of Aristotle Volume Two Part One: Notes*, Internet Archive (download)

Judt, Tony (2010) *Ill Fares the Land: A Treatise On Our Present Discontents*, Allen Lane

Kay, John (2009) *Narrow Banking: The Reform of Banking Regulation*, Centre for the Study of Financial Innovation

_____ (2015) *Other People's Money: Masters of the Universe or Servants of the People?* Profile Books

Kelly, Marjorie (2012) *Owning Our Future: The Emerging Ownership Revolution*, Berrett-Koehler

Kennedy, Margrit (2012) *Occupy Money: Creating an Economy Where Everybody Wins*, New Society

Kerridge, Eric (1991) *Trade and Banking in Early Modern England*, Manchester University Press

Keynes, John Maynard (1923) *A Tract on Monetary Reform*, Macmillan

_____ (1930) *A Treatise on Money*, Harcourt Brace

_____ (1932) "Economic Possibilities for our Grandchildren" in *Essays in Persuasion*, Harcourt Brace

_____ (1933) *Essays*, Internet Archive (download)

_____ (2008) *The General Theory of Employment, Interest and Money*, BN Publishing

Kindleberger, Charles (1999) *Manias, Panics and Crashes: A History of Financial Crises*, Basic Books

_____ (2007) *A Financial History of Western Europe*, Routledge

King, Mervyn (2016) *The End of Alchemy: Money, Banking and the Future of the Global Economy*, Little, Brown

Kinzer, Stephen (2006) *Overthrow: America's century of regime change from Hawaii to Iraq*, Times Books/Henry Holt

Kleer, Richard (2008) '"Fictitious Cash": English Public Finance and Paper Money, 1689-97' in *Money, Power, and Print: Interdisciplinary studies on the financial revolution in the British Isles*, ed. Charles Ivar McGrath and Chris Fauske, University of Delaware Press

Klein, Naomi (2017) *No Is Not Enough*, Haymarket Books

Kotlikoff, Laurence J. (2011) *Jimmy Stewart is Dead: Ending the World's Ongoing Financial Plague with Limited Purpose Banking*, Wiley

Kramer, Alan (1991) *The West German Economy, 1945-1955*, Berg

Kramer, Samuel Noah (1969) *Cradle of Civilization*, Little, Brown

_____ (1988) *History Begins at Sumer*, University of Pennsylvania Press

Kramnick, Isaac (1992) *Bolingbroke and his Circle: The politics of nostalgia in the age of Walpole*, Cornell University Press

Kumhof (2013) *The Chicago Plan Revisited*, IMF

Kurtzman, Joel (1994) *The Death of Money: How Electronic Economy Has Destabilised the World's Market and Created Economic Chaos*, Little Brown

Kyd, (1795) *A Treatise on The Law Of Bills Of Exchange and Promissory Notes*, Internet Archive (download)

Lamb, Samuel (1659) 'Seasonable Observations Humbly Offered To His Highness The Lord Protector' reprinted in *Somers' Tracts Volume vi* P.454 ff. Internet Archive (download)

Lanchester, John (2010) *Whoops! Why everyone owes everyone and no one can pay*, Allen Lane

Latouche, Robert (2013) *The Birth Of Western Economy*, Routledge

Law, John (1705) *Money and Trade Considered...* Internet Archive (download)

Lawrence, William H. (2019) *Understanding Negotiable Instruments and Payment Systems,* Carolina Academic

Leao, D. F. & Rhodes, P. J. (2016) *The Laws of Solon: A New Edition*, I.B. Tauris

Lee, Ian B. (2005) 'Is There a Cure for Corporate "Psychopathy"?' in *American Business Law Journal*

Lekachman, Robert (1959) *A History of Economic Ideas,* Harper

_____ (1975) *Economists at Bay*, McGraw-Hill Inc

Lerner, Gerda (1986) *The Creation of Patriarchy*, Oxford University Press

Lester, Richard A. (1939) *Monetary Experiments*, David & Charles (new ed)

Levett, A. Elizabeth (1928) *English Economic History*, Ernest Benn

Lietaer, Bernard (2013) *Rethinking Money: How New Currencies Turn Scarcity into Prosperity*, Berrett-Koehler

Lilothia, L. (2010) *Fundamentals of Credit Creation in Banking,* Cyber Tech

Lim, Betty (2019) *Social Movements Powering the Future of Money*, Kindle

Lipson, Ephraim (1937-43) *The Economic History of England. Volumes I-III,* Adam & Charles

_____ (1944) *Europe 1914-1939* A & C Black

_____ (1949) *The Growth of English Society: A short economic history*, A & C Black

_____ (2009) *The Economic History of England Vol III: The Age of Mercantilism*, Cornell

List, Friedrich (1827a) 'Professor List's Speech', Delivered at the Philadelphia Manufacturers' Dinner, Internet Archive (download)

_____ (1827b) *Outlines of American Political Economy in a Series of Letters,* Philadelphia

_____ (1856) *The National System Of Political Economy*, trans. Matile, Internet Archive (download)

_____ (1904) *The National System Of Political Economy* trans. S.S. Lloyd, Longman

Locke, John, (1690) *Two Treatises Of Government*, Internet Archive (download)

_____ (1991) *Locke**Error! Bookmark not defined.**, John, 1632-1704 Locke on money.* (ed. P. H. Kelly) Clarendon

Lonergan, Eric (2014) *Money* (second revised ed.) Routledge

Luyendijk, Joris (2016) *Swimming with Sharks: Inside the World of the Bankers*, Guardian Faber

Lyotard, Jean-Francois (2015) *Libidinal Economy*, Bloomsbury Academic

Magnani, Esteban (2009) *The Silent Change: Recovered Businesses in Argentina*, Editorial Teseo

Mahmoud, Mohsen S. (2011) *Money Creation and Slavery of Debt*, America Star Books

Maitland, F.W. (1911) *The Collected Papers, Vols I-III* Internet Archive (download)

Maitland, F.W. (2003) ed. David Runciman & Magnus Ryan Maitland: *State, Trust and Corporation*, Cambridge University Press

Malynes, Gerard de (1601) *A Treatise of the Canker of England's Commonwealth*, Internet Archive (download).

_____ (1622) *The Maintenance of Free Trade*, Internet Archive (download).

Mann, Michael (2005) *Incoherent Empire*, Verso Books.

Mantoux, P. (1970) *Industrial Revolution in the Eighteenth Century*, Methuen

Martin, J.B. (1892) *The Grasshopper in Lombard Street*, Internet Archive (download).

Marx, Karl, (1887) *Capital*, download from Marxists.org

Massy, Charles (2018) *Call of the Reed Warbler* Chelsea Green

McMillan, Jonathan (2014) *The End of Banking: Money, Credit, and the Digital Revolution* Zero/One Economics

McNally, David (2014) *Global Slump: The Economics and Politics of Crisis and Resistance*, PM Press

Mereness, Newton D. (1901) *Maryland as a Proprietary Province*, Internet Archive (download)

Mill, J. S. (1965) *Principles of Political Economy Vols 1 and 2*, Liberty Fund

Miller, H. E. (2011) *Banking Theories in the United States Before 1860*, LLC

Mints, Lloyd W. (1945) *A History of Banking Theory in Great Britain and the United States*, University of Chicago Press

_____ (1950) *Monetary Policy for A Competitive Society*, McGraw-Hill

Mitchell, B.R. (1988) *British Historical Statistics*, Cambridge University Press

Mokyr, J (ed) (2003) *The Oxford Encyclopedia of Economic History*, Oxford University Press

Monbiot, George (2000) *Captive State: The Corporate Takeover of Britain*, Macmillan

Monroe, Arthur Eli (2014) *Monetary Theory before Adam Smith*, Harvard University Press

Montesquieu, Baron de (1748) *De l'Esprit des Lois*, Internet Archive (download)

Mosley, Ivo (2013) *In the Name of the People*, Imprint Academic

Muldrew, Craig (1998) *The Economy of Obligation: The culture of credit and social relations in early modern England*, Macmillan Press

Mun, Thomas (1694) 'England's Treasure By Forraign Trade' Wikisource (download)

Munro, John H. (1991) 'The International Law Merchant' in *Banchi pubblici, banchi privati e monti di pietà*, Società ligure di storia patria

_____ (1994) *Textiles, Towns and Trade: essays in the economic history of late medieval England and the Low Countries*, Variorum

_____ (2003) 'The Medieval Origins of the Financial Revolution: Usury, Rentes, and Negotiability', *The International History Review*

Murphy, Antoin E. (2009) *The Genesis of Macroeconomics: New ideas from Sir William Petty to Henry Thornton*, Oxford University Press

Namier, Lewis (1957) *The Structure of Politics At The Ascension of George III*, Palgrave Macmillan

Nathan, Otto (1971) *The Nazi Economic System: Germany's Mobilization for War*, Russell & Russell

Neal, Larry (2015) *A Concise History of International Finance*, Cambridge University Press

Nef, John U. (1950) *War and Human Progress: An essay on the rise of industrial civilization*, Routledge & K. Paul

Neild, R. (2002) *Public Corruption: The Dark Side of Social Evolution*, Anthem

Nelson, Benjamin (1969) *The Idea of Usury: From Tribal Brotherhood to Universal Otherhood*, University of Chicago Press

Nicholson, C. E. (1994) *Writing and the Rise of Finance: Capital satires of the early eighteenth century,* Cambridge University Press

Nokes, David (1987) *Raillery and Rage: A Study of Eighteenth Century Satire,* Palgrave Macmillan

O'Malley, Michael (2012) *Face Value: The Entwined Histories of Money and Race in America,* University of Chicago Press

Oakeshott, Michael (1991) 'The Political Economy of Freedom' in *Rationalism in Politics and Other Essays,* Liberty Fund

_____ (1999) 'The Rule of Law' in *On History and Other Essays,* Liberty Fund

OEEH (The Oxford Encyclopedia of Economic History) (2003) Oxford University Press

Overy, R.J. (2008) *The Nazi Economic Recovery,* Cambridge University Press

Paddock, Richard C., (2016) 'Banker Brother of Malaysian Premier Steps Aside From Posts Amid Inquiry', *New York Times,* 18 April

Paget's Law of Banking (1922) available online

Paine, W. W. (1930) *Banking,* Ernest Benn

Palmer, R. R. (1959) *The Age of Democratic Revolution: A Political History Of America, 1760-1800, Volume 1 The Challenge,* Princeton University Press

Palmer, Vernon V. (1989) 'The History of Privity - The Formative Period (1500-1680)' in *The American Journal of Legal History,* Vol. 33, No. 1

Parks, Tim (2005) *Medici Money: Banking, metaphysics and art in fifteenth-century Florence,* Profile Books

Passingham, W.J. (1935) *London's Markets, Their Origin and History,* Sampson Row

Pells, Rachael, (2017) 'Government begins plans to sell off billions of pounds worth of student debt to private companies', *The Independent,* 6 February, www.bit.ly/TPbr21

Perkins, John (2005) *Confessions of an Economic Hitman,* Ebury Press

_____ (2016) *The New Confessions of an Economic Hit Man: The shocking story of how America really took over the world,* Berrett-Koehler

Persky, Joseph (2007) 'From Usury To Interest' in *Journal of Economic Perspectives*

Petty, Sir William (1799) *Tracts; Chiefly Relating to Ireland,* Internet Archive (download)

_____ (1899) *Economic Writings, Vols I & II,* Internet Archive (download)

_____ *Essays on Mankind and Political Arithmetic* (Kindle)

Pezzolo, Luciano, (2004) 'Bonds and government debt in Italian city-states, 1250-1650' in *The Origins of Value: The financial innovations that created modern capital markets* ed. W. N. Goetzmann and K. G. Rouwenhorst, Oxford University Press

Phillips, C.A. (1931) *Bank Credit*, Internet Archive (download)

_____ (1937) *Banking and the Business Cycle*, Internet Archive (download)

Piergiovanni, Vito (1993) *The Growth of the Bank as Institution and the Development of Money-Business Law*, Duncker & Humblot

Pirenne, Henri (1948) *A History of Europe*, George Allen & Unwin

_____ (1969) *Medieval Cities*, Princeton University Press

Plucknett, Theodore F.T. (2010) *A Concise History of the Common Law*, Liberty Fund

Pocock, J. G. A. (2003) *The Machiavellian Moment: Florentine Political Thought and the Atlantic Republican Tradition*, Princeton Univ. Press

Pomerantsev, Peter (2015) *Nothing is True and Everything is Possible: Adventures in Modern Russia*, Faber & Faber

Poovey, Mary (2008) *Genres of the Credit Economy: mediating value in eighteenth- and nineteenth-century Britain*, University of Chicago Press

Postan. M.M. (1973) *Medieval Trade and Finance*, Cambridge Univ. Press

Pruessner, A.H. (1928) 'The Earliest Traces of Negotiable Instruments' in *The American Journal of Semitic Languages and Literatures*, Vol. 44, No. 2

Radford, R.A. (1945) 'The Economic Organisation of a P.O.W. Camp' in *Economica*

Ravenstone, Piercy (1966) *Thoughts on the Funding System and its Effects*, Augustus M. Kelley

_____ (2011) *A Few Doubts on the Subjects of Population and Political Economy*, Augustus M. Kelley

Raworth, Kate (2018) *Doughnut Economics: Seven Ways to Think Like a 21st-Century Economist*, Random House Business

Raymond, Daniel (1823) *The Elements of Political Economy In Two Volumes*. Augustus M. Kelley (reprint, 1964) available at www.bit.ly/TPbr30

Reinert, Sophus A. (2011) *Translating Empire: emulation and the origins of political economy*, Harvard University Press

Ressler, Peter (2011) *Conversations with Wall Street: The Inside Story of the Financial Armageddon & How to Prevent the Next One*, Bookmaster

Ricardo, David *The Works and Correspondence of David Ricardo* 11 vols, Liberty Fund online

Richards, R. D. (1958) *The Early History of Banking in England*, Cass

Ricks, Morgan (2016) *The Money Problem: Rethinking Financial Regulation*, University of Chicago Press

Ritschl, Albrecht (1996) 'Sustainability of High Public Debt: What the Historical Record Shows' in *Swedish Economic Policy Review*. Available on Researchgate

Roberts, Keith, (2011) *The origins of business, money, and markets*, Columbia University Press

Robertson, D.H. (1944) *Money*, Nisbet

_____ (1959) *Lectures on Economic Principles*, Staples Press

Robertson, J. & Bunzl, J. (2004) *Monetary Reform – Making it Happen!*, ISPO

Robinson, Joan (1967) *Economics: an awkward corner*, Pantheon Books

_____ (1970) *Freedom and Necessity: Introduction to the Study of Society* Allen & Unwin

Robinson, Joan (1971) *Economic Heresies*, Basic Books

_____ (1981) *What are the Questions and Other Essays: Further Contributions to Modern Economics*, Routledge

_____ (2013) *The Accumulation of Capital*, Palgrave Macmillan

_____ (2014) *Contributions to Modern Economics*, Academic Press

Roebuck, Derek (1991) *The Background of the Common Law*, Oxford University Press

_____ (2013) *Mediation and Arbitration in the Middle Ages: England 1154 to 1558*, Holo Books

Rogers, J. E. T. (1909) *The Economic Interpretation of History*, G. Putnam's Sons

Rogers, James H. (1933) 'The Absorption of Bank Credit' in *Econometrica*

_____ (1938) *Capitalism in Crisis*, Yale University Press

Rogers, James S. (2010) *The Early History of the Law of Bills and Notes: A Study of the Origins of Anglo-American Commercial Law*, Cambridge University Press

_____ (2012) *The End of Negotiable Instruments*, Oxford University Press

Rogers, Thorold (1887) *The First Nine Years of the Bank of England*, Internet Archive (download).

Roseveare, Henry (1991) *The Financial Revolution 1660-1760*, Longman

Rostovzeff, Michael Ivanovitch (1926) *The Social & Economic History of the Roman Empire*, Clarendon Press

Rothbard, Murray N. (2002) *History of Money and Banking in the United States: The Colonial Era to World War II*, Ludwig von Mises Institute

_____ (2010) *Austrian Perspective on the History of Economic Thought*, Ludwig von Mises Institute

_____ (2011) *The Mystery of Banking*, Terra Libertas

Routh, Guy (1989) *The Origin of Economic Ideas*, Palgrave Macmillan

Rowbotham, Michael (1998) *The Grip of Death: A Study of Modern Money, Debt Slavery and Destructive Economics*, Jon Carpenter

Russell, Conrad (1974) *The Crisis of Parliaments 1509-1660*, Oxford University Press

Ryan-Collins, Josh (2012) *Where Does Money Come From?: A Guide to the UK Monetary & Banking System*, NEF

Sampson, Anthony (2005) *Who Runs This Place?: The Anatomy of Britain in the 21st Century*, John Murray

Saw, Reginald (1945) *The Bank of England, 1694-1944*, Harrap

Sayers, R.S. (1967) *Modern Banking*, Oxford University Press

Schacht, H. Horace Greeley (1979) *The Stabilization of the Mark*, Arno Press

Schlichter, Detlev, (2011) *Paper Money Collapse*, Wiley

Schumpeter, J.A (1939) *Business Cycles Vols 1 and 2*, McGraw-Hill

_____ (1954) *History of Economic Analysis,* Allen & Unwin

_____ (2008) *Capitalism, Socialism and Democracy*, Harper Perennial

Schwarzschild, Leopold (1986) *Red Prussian: Life and Legend of Karl Marx*, Pickwick Books

Schweitzer, Mary M. (1989) 'State-Issued Currency and the Ratification of the U.S. Constitution' in *The Journal of Economic History*

Scott, Tom (2012) *The City-State in Europe, 1000-1600: Hinterland, Territory, Region*, Oxford University Press

Scrutton, Thomas E. (2008) *Commons and Common Fields*, BiblioBazaar

_____ (2009) *Land in Fetters*, General Books

Sealy, L. S. and Hooley, R. J. A. (1999) *Text and Materials in Commercial Law*, Butterworths Law

Selgin, George A. (1988) *The Theory of Free Banking*, Rowman & Littlefield

Senior, Nassau William (1882) *Conversations and Journals in Egypt Vol.2*, Internet Archive (download)

Silverman, Dan P. (1998) *Hitler's Economy: Nazi work creation programs, 1933-1936*, Harvard University Press

Silverman, Peter (2000) *Reconstructing Europe After the Great War*, Harvard University Press

Simons, Henry C. (1948) *Economic Policy for a Free Society*, University of Chicago Press. Also available at www.bit.ly/TPbr26

Singh, Kavaljit (2008) *Taking It Private: The Global Consequences of Private Equity*, The Corner House Briefing 37

Smart, P.E. & Chorley, R. S. T. (1990) *Leading Cases in the Law of Banking*, Sweet & Maxwell

Smith, Adam (1776) *An Inquiry into the Nature and Causes of the Wealth of Nations*, Internet Archive (download)

_____ (1896) *Lectures on Justice, Police, Revenue and Arms*, Internet Archive (download)

Smith, Preserved (1948) *The Age Of The Reformation*, Henry Holt

Smith, Vera C. (1990) *The Rationale of Central Banking, and the Free Banking Alternative*, Liberty Fund

Soto, Hernando De (2000) *The Mystery of Capital*, Bantam Press

Sowell, Thomas (1999) *Conquests and Cultures: An International History*, Basic Books

Speck, W. A. (1977) *Stability and Strife: England, 1714-60*, Hodder Arnold

Spufford, Peter (2006) *Power and Profit: The Merchant in Medieval Europe*, Thames Hudson

Stapleton, J. (1995) *Group Rights: Perspectives Since 1900*, St Augustine's Press

Stasavage, David (2015) *States of Credit: Size, Power, and the Development of European Polities*, Princeton University Press

Steensland, Brian (2007) *The Failed Welfare Revolution: America's Struggle over Guaranteed Income Policy*, Princeton University Press

Steiner, George A. (1942) *Economic Problems of War*, John Wiley

Steinmetz, Greg (2015) *The Richest Man Who Ever Lived: The Life and Times of Jacob Fugger*, Simon & Schuster

Stone, Lawrence & Stone, Jeanne C. Fawtier (1984) *An Open Elite? England, 1540-1880*, Oxford University Press

Story, Joseph (1868) *Commentaries on The Law Of Promissory Notes*, Internet Archive (download)

Supple, Barry E. (1963) *The Experience of Economic Growth*, Random House

Szanto, Andras (2008) *What Orwell Didn't Know: Propaganda and the New Face of American Politics*, Public Affairs

Tawney, R. H. & Eileen Power (eds) (1965) *Tudor Economic Documents: Being Select Documents Illustrating the Economic and Social History of Tudor England*, Longman

Tawney, R.H. (1967) *Agrarian Problem in the Sixteenth Century*, Torchbooks

Taylor, James (2014) *Creating Capitalism: Joint-Stock Enterprise in British Politics and Culture, 1800-1870* Royal Historical Society

Taylor, John of Caroline (1794) *An Enquiry into Principles and Tendency of Certain Public Measures*, Internet Archive (download)

_____ (1814) *An Inquiry into the Principles and Policy of the Government of the United States*, Internet Archive (download)

_____ (1822) *Tyranny Unmasked*, Liberty Fund edition 1992

_____ (1820) *Construction Construed*, Internet Archive (download)

Temperley, H.W.V. (1908) 'The Revolution and the Revolution Settlement in Great Britain' in *Cambridge Modern History Vol 5*, Cambridge Univ. Press

The Cambridge Economic History of Europe, Cambridge University Press

Thirsk, Joan (1974) *Seventeenth Century Economic Documents*, Oxford University Press

_____ (1989) *Economic Policy and Projects: Development of a Consumer Society in Early Modern England*, Clarendon Paperbacks

_____ (2003) *The Rural Economy of England*, Hambledon Continuum

Thorne, W. J. (1948) *Banking*, Oxford University Press

Tilden, Freeman (1936) *A World in Debt*, Internet Archive (download)

Tooze, Adam (2007) *The Wages of Destruction: The Making and Breaking of the Nazi Economy*, Penguin

Trevelyan, G.M. (1978) *English Social History*, Longman

UNESCO (2018) *Unesco's Commitment to Biodiversity: Connecting People and Nature for an Inspiring Future*

Usher, Abbott Payson (1934) 'The Origins of Banking: The Primitive Bank of Deposit, 1200-1600' in *The Economic History Review*

_____ (1943) *The Early History of Deposit Banking in Mediterranean Europe*, Harvard University Press

_____ (2010) *An Introduction to the Industrial History of England*, Nabu Press

Valenze, Deborah (2006) *The Social Life of Money in the English Past*, Cambridge University Press

Van De Mieroop, Marc (1999) *Cuneiform Texts and the Writing of History*, Routledge

_____ (2006) *History of the Ancient Near East: Ca. 3000-323 BC*, John Wiley

Van Horn, Robert (2014) 'A Note on Henry Simons' Death', *History of Political Economy 46 (3)*

Van Lerven, Frank (2015) *Would There be Enough Credit in a Sovereign Money System?*, Positive Money

Varoufakis, Yanis (2017) *And the Weak Suffer What They Must?: Europe, Austerity and the Threat to Global Stability*, Vintage

Vickers, Douglas (2012) *Studies in the Theory of Money 1690-1776*, LLC

Von Mises, Ludwig (1981) *The Theory of Money and Credit*, Liberty Fund

Wade, John, (1831) *The Black Book*, Google Books (download)

Walker, Amasa (1866) *The Science of Wealth*, Internet Archive (download)

Walker, Francis A. (1888) *Political Economy*, Internet Archive (download)

Wallich, Henry (1955) *Mainsprings of the German Revival*, Yale Univ. Press

Ward, A.W. & Prothero, G.W. & Leathes, S. (eds.) (1908) *The Cambridge Modern History*, Cambridge University Press

Webb, Steven Benjamin (1989) *Hyperinflation and Stabilization in Weimar Germany*, Oxford University Press

Weber, M. (1930) *The Protestant Ethic and the Spirit of Capitalism*, Allen & Unwin

_____ (1961) *General Economic History*, Collier Books

Wedel, Janine (2011) *Shadow Elite: How the World's New Power Brokers Undermine Democracy, Government and the Free Market*, Basic Books

Wennerlind, Carl (2011) *Casualties of Credit: The English Financial Revolution, 1620-1720*, Harvard University Press

Werner, Richard (2005) *The New Paradigm in Macroeconomics: Solving the Riddle of Japanese Macroeconomic Performance*, Palgrave Macmillan

_____ (2014) 'How Do Banks Create Money, And Why Can Other Firms Not Do The Same?' *International Review of Financial Analysis 36*

_____ (2016) 'A lost century in economics: Three theories of banking and the conclusive evidence' *International Review of Financial Analysis*

White, Eugene N. (2004) 'From Privatized to Government-Administered Tax Collection: Tax Farming in Eighteenth Century France' in *The Economic History Review*, Vol. 57, No. 4

White, Andrew Dickson (1959) *Fiat Money Inflation in France*, Foundation for Economic Education

White, Lawrence (1992) *Competition and Currency*, New York Univ. Press

Wicksell, Knut (1936) *Interest and Prices*, Macmillan

Wiener, Norbert (1961) Cybernbetics, MIT Press

_____ (1966) *God and Golem, Inc.* MIT Press

_____ (1988) *The Human Use of Human Beings,* Da Capo

Wilson, Charles (1969) *Economic History and the Historian: Collected Essays,* Littlehampton Book Services

_____ (1976) *Transformation of Europe, 1558-1648*, Littlehampton Book Services

_____ (1978) *Profit and Power*, Springer

_____ (1985) *England's Apprenticeship, 1603-1763* Longman

Wilson, Thomas, (1925) *A discourse upon usury by way of dialogue and orations, for the better variety and more delight of all those that shall read this treatise* [1572], G. Bell & Sons

Withers, Hartley (1920a) *International Finance*, John Murray

_____ (1920b) *The Case for Capitalism*, Nash & Grayson

_____ (1923) *The Meaning of Money*, John Murray

_____ (1924) *Bankers & Credit*, Nash & Grayson

_____ (1931) *Everybody's Business*, Jonathan Cape

_____ (1932) *Money in the Melting Pot*, Sidgwick & Jackson

Wolf, Martin (2015) *The Shifts and the Shocks: What we've learned – and have still to learn – from the financial crisis*, Penguin

Wood, Andy (2001) *Riot, Rebellion and Popular Politics in Early Modern England*, Palgrave

Wu, C-Y (2010) An Outline of International Price Theories, Routledge

Zagorin, Perez (1969) *Court and the Country: Beginning of the English Revolution*, Law Book Co of Australasia

Zimmermann, Reinhard (1996) *The Law of Obligations*, Clarendon Press

Index

About the Author

Born in 1951, Ivo Mosley is married with 4 children and 4.5 grandchildren. He has a degree in Japanese from Oxford University and an MA in Musical Theatre from Goldsmiths College. He lived for 25 years in Devon before moving to London. After a versatile career writing books and articles on current affairs, philosophy, poetry and politics (and five pieces of musical theatre) he began to write about the crisis affecting our world today.

His first book on this subject concerned the dubious nature of democracy. *In the Name of the People* pointed out a fact long evident to political philosophers: that voting for representatives named by powerful political parties is not 'rule by the people'.

He then turned to the money system which underpins our current crisis. In *Bank Robbery*, the result of seven years' work, he exposes the unassailable powers that rule (and are destroying) our world today.

Other work by Ivo Mosley:

2017: ***Mad King Suibhne,*** opera libretto, music by Noah Mosley. Produced at Bury Court Opera, at Lilian Bayliss House (ENO) and at Messum's Wiltshire. "A succinctly poetic libretto" *Opera Magazine* (Yehuda Shapiro). "Tremendously enjoyable and accomplished" Rupert Christiansen.

2013: ***In the Name of the People*** (Imprint Academic). "A … scathing critique of representative government", Book News Inc.

2008: ***The London Buskers Orchestra Meet for the End of the World***, play-with-music. First performed at Battersea Arts Centre.

2007: ***London Stories,*** play-with-music, first performed at Goldsmith's College, London. Life (and death) in London across 2000 years. Words Ivo Mosley, music Kevin Richardson.

2006: ***Frida and Diego,*** musical drama, first performed at Goldsmith's College, London. Words Ivo Mosley, music traditional Mexican. The lives of Frida Kahlo and Diego Rivera. Also workshopped at RADA. 2007.

2003: ***Democracy, Fascism & the New World Order*** (Imprint Academic). A look at the political oligarchy who control us in the name of democracy and freedom. "Provocative Stuff!" – Andrew Morrod, *Daily Mail.*

2002: ***Science,*** a musical drama, first performed at the Bridewell Theatre, London. Words and music by Ivo Mosley. A story about modern science and the search for eternal life.

2000: ***Dumbing Down*** (Imprint Academic). Essays on cultural change and malaise. "At last – a guide to the moronic inferno!" Laurence Coupe in *PNR.*

1999: ***Danny's Dream,*** first performed at the Rowntree Theatre York. Words by Ivo Mosley, music by Piers Browne. "A raw and truthful show... The songs fizz with anger, hurt and resentment – but love and humour too." Charles Hutchinson, *Yorkshire Evening Press.*

1993: ***The Green Book of Poetry*** (Frontier Publishing), re-published in 1996 as *Earth Poems* (HarperSanFrancisco). An anthology of hundreds of poems from around the world, many translated by Ivo, with commentary. "A book for our time" *The Weekend Telegraph.* "This book should be open on everyone's kitchen table" *Village Voice.* "A book to possess!" Naomi Lewis, *London Evening Standard.* "Book of the Year" Raymond Carr, *The Spectator.* "Brilliant and idiosyncratic... entirely fascinating" Polly Devlin, *The Week.* "One of the best anthologies – ever!" Brendan Kennelly.

About the Publisher

Triarchy Press is a small, independent publisher of books that bring a wider, systemic or contextual approach to many different areas of life, including:

The Money System
(Bernard Lietaer, Margrit Kennedy, Maria Pereira, John Rogers and others)

Government, Education, Health and other public services
(John Seddon, Simon Guilfoyle, Margaret Hannah and others)

Ecology, Sustainability and Regenerative Cultures
(Nora Bateson, Daniel Wahl and others)

Leading and Managing Organisations
(Russ Ackoff, Barry Oshry, Bill Tate and others)

Psychotherapy and Arts and other Expressive Therapies
(Mary Booker, Bob Chisholm and others)

Walking, Psychogeography and Mythogeography
(Phil Smith, Roy Bayfield, Ernesto Pujol and others)

Movement and Somatics
(Sandra Reeve, Sarah Whatley, Katya Bloom, Margit Galanter and others)

The Future and Future Studies
(Graham Leicester, Bill Sharpe, Patricia Lustig and others)

For more information, please visit:

www.triarchypress.net